CRICKET

CRICKET

Selected and edited by

ADRIENNE SIMPSON

HarperCollins*Publishers New Zealand*

By the same author

Opera in New Zealand — Aspects of History and Performance (editor)

Southern Voices — International Opera Singers of New Zealand
(with Peter Downes)

The Greatest Ornaments of their Profession:
the New Zealand Tours by the Simonsen Opera Companies

Opera's Farthest Frontier: A History of Professional Opera in New Zealand

First published 1996
HarperCollins*Publishers (New Zealand) Limited*
P.O. Box 1, Auckland

ISBN 1 86950 221 3

Cover photo of Adam Parore by Andrew Cornaga, Photosport
Cover designed by Craig Humberstone
Designed by Craig Humberstone; typeset by Steve Ballantyne
Printed by HarperCollins Hong Kong

CONTENTS

Dedicated to the cricket lovers among my family and friends —
Nicky Chilton, Richard Fraser, Anna Rogers, Ian Watt, Dennis Wilson
and Lawrie Wright.

FOREWORD

'Cricket transcends the individual. It has a life of its own and in interaction with it the humblest of us may be raised to a kind of greatness, the most domineering be reduced to a nullity,' wrote C.L.R James, arguably cricket's finest author. How true, and its greatest joy is that it attracts people of so many cultures, classes and walks of life. Many of our greatest writers are ardent devotees, and a glittering kaleidoscope have faithfully and beautifully recorded the game in prose and poetry: J.M. Barrie, Siegfried Sassoon, Cecil Day Lewis, Edmund Blunden, A.E. Housman, A.G. Macdonnell, Herbert and Emily Farjeon, A.A. Milne, E.V. Lucas, Anthony Trollope and William Blake, to name but a few. Musicians, painters and scholars of all disciplines do not escape the net and one of these, Adrienne Simpson, has been a willing captive of cricket for many years. Mention her name and people will tell you that she writes and talks about music and opera in New Zealand and Australia, and has published several highly regarded books on opera. Equally important is her deep love of sport and, in particular, cricket. She played the game with modest success as a girl and since those days has been an avid but discerning reader, watcher and listener. Ms Simpson has taken a giant step further and has assembled material from her favourite writers from New Zealand and overseas to provide an anthology relating solely to our own cricket and cricketers.

Until recently the sources of cricket anthologies have been England and Australia, but there are sufficient writers of quality in New Zealand, and more than enough material, to justify our own books. The highly respected

Ron Palenski produced a fine collection of cricket stories in *Bat and Pad*, a modest production which came and went without the recognition which it richly deserved.

Some of the writers included here are acknowledged authorities on cricket, others are gifted journalists and authors who write about the game occasionally because they love it.

Of the overseas writers John Arlott is obviously a favourite, and his prolific pen is prominent, with contributions on the widely contrasting 1949 and 1958 New Zealand teams. Writing in 1983, he also chooses his best New Zealand team. Few would quibble with his selection, and only Martin Crowe would be an automatic addition since that date, although the selection of Mooney or Wadsworth as keeper would be open to challenge.

It was a delight for me to discover four of my special favourites. R.C. Robertson Glasgow, affectionately known as Robinson Crusoe, is here. (It was Charlie McGahey, the old Essex pro, who, returning to the dressing room having made a swift 0 against Somerset and asked what had happened, exclaimed: 'Bowled first ball by an old b...I thought was dead two thousand years ago, Robinson Crusoe!'). His writing can be summed up in his own words: 'I have always laughed when playing cricket, except when slip fielders showed signs of lumbago, and I saw no reason to stop laughing when I wrote about it.' Appropriately his subject is Tom Lowry, a Somerset colleague. Ian Peebles is another delightful raconteur with whom I had the pleasure of dining at Martin Donnelly's home in Sydney many years ago. He recounted his hilarious experiences while touring India under Lord Tennyson in the days of the British Raj. There is no more respected writer than Johnny Woodcock, another charming dinner companion, while the fourth of my favourites is A.A. Thomson. Anyone who can choose *Pavilioned in Splendour* as a title for a cricket book earns a special place. As a small boy, hearing this line from the hymn *O Worship the King* for the first time, Thomson had visions of Lord Hawke resplendent in golden coronet gazing down from his throne in some celestial long room.

Included in the anthology are pertinent extracts from players' autobiographies and biographies, including Bert Sutcliffe, John Reid, Glenn Turner, Ian Smith, Ken Rutherford, Bruce Edgar and Jeremy Coney. The first two, close friends, provide nostalgic reading for me, whilst Coney is one of a rare breed of sportspersons who can play, write and speak with distinction.

Predictably and appropriately New Zealand's professional cricket critics Dick Brittenden, Don Cameron and Ron Palenski feature prominently, as does Terry McLean, who writes so well about so many sports beyond rugby.

BBC commentator Don Mosey, who had a passionate love affair with New Zealand, is also included, writing contrastingly of Pukekura Park and Eden Park's 'Cans Corner'.

The editor's real discernment is highlighted in her selection of a distinguished group of journalists, including Warwick Roger and Spiro Zavos, and it is significant that almost without exception they have been drawn from contributions to *Metro* and to a lesser extent the *Listener*. I remember judging articles submitted in a national sporting journalists' competition on two separate occusions years ago, and Warwick Roger won by a wide margin each time.

From the women's dressing room comes Elizabeth Smither, whom we got to know well when Michael Smither was the Frances Hodgkins Fellow and they were neighbours both at Patearoa and in Dunedin, and Nancy Joy. The latter's description of her 1949 tour of New Zealand with the England women's team was for me an unhappy inclusion. It provides a description of Otago's defeat by an innings and 316 runs in less than two days — I was Otago's coach!

There is no Cardus or Batchelor, which in the case of Cardus seems surprising at first glance. It could not have been that the editor regards him with the same suspicion as did 'Ticker' Mitchell, the famous Yorkshire character, who echoed the sentiments of many old English pros when he said, 'I think nowt of thy writings, Mr Cardus; they be too flowery for me'. No, not with their shared passion for music and cricket! I imagine that there was nothing adequate or appropriate available relating to New Zealand, for Cardus's best writing was done before the war when, in particular, his descriptions of the 'Wars of the Roses' and the Ashes series were superb.

The choice of subjects is also discerning, and again I am delighted that Sutcliffe and Donnelly have such a significant presence, simply because there have been no post-war left-handers of greater quality, charm and modesty. Furthermore, they were involved in two of New Zealand's, and in fact cricket's, greatest achievements against the clock, and both are dealt with in detail. What need is there for all the synthetic gimmicks introduced to encourage more spectator support when, in 1949, New Zealand compiled 153 in 58 minutes against Lancashire, who raced through 26 overs, and 109 in 28 minutes (Donnelly and Sutcliffe 50 in 11 minutes) while Hampshire raced through 12 overs.

Dunedin-born Clarrie Grimmett also features prominently, and I had the pleasure of discussing his biography with its author Ashley Mallett in Adelaide a year or two ago. Walter Hadlee, unchallenged as my best cricket captain, receives proper recognition from Arlott, and Spiro Zavos chooses my greatest cricket hero, Keith Miller, as a central figure.

Finally, Ms Simpson, after guiding us pleasantly through a variety of themes, ends the anthology by outlining in more detail her interests in cricket, including an encounter with another charming character, Frank Gilligan. He also umpired my matches against Wanganui Collegiate, where he was headmaster for many years, and I treasured his advice on legside technique.

An avid collector of every available cricket book before and immediately after the Second World War, I became markedly less enthusiastic as more and more journalists and players produced routine tales of overseas tours to the extent that sometimes three or four books would appear covering a single tour. Added to this, ghosted autobiographies or biographies of prominent players and ex-players were churned out with alarming frequency. Today, my purchases are rigorously restrictive, and it is therefore always a pleasure to locate an anthology of cricket where the writings are selected and edited by those with a genuine love for and knowledge of the game. There are consequently a significant number of such volumes in my cricket library which can be happily reread and to which I turn surprisingly frequently for reference purposes. Adrienne Simpson's will be a welcome addition and, if this is her first contribution to cricket literature, I certainly hope that it will not be her last.

Iain Gallaway
July 1996

PREFACE

The pieces in this anthology were selected to illustrate particular themes, rather than to be a comprehensive history of New Zealand cricket. Trying to choose just a few items from the wealth of material available was not easy, but it was very enjoyable and led to many unexpected and pleasurable discoveries. The final choice of what to include was a matter of personal preference. I particularly liked all these pieces — and I hope you will too.

Adrienne Simpson
Wellington, May 1996

ONE

LEARNING THE GAME

How does the love of cricket begin? Those who play the game well usually seem to encounter it at an early age. Having at least one parent with a passion for the sport must be a great help, since skills are often developed more easily in the intimacy of the family setting. Some of the world's more epic matches probably took place just outside the back door.

Our backyard was often a hive of competition — summers of schoolboys, cousins, neighbours and city council workmen who would flock to our tennis court to relive a turbulent tied test. Even when these crowds deserted us, the family game remained intact. We all had our parts to play. Mother excelled in cries of encouragement from the kitchen window, while my two brothers and my father closed in as they eagerly sensed their turn to bat.

Even now Father is tall; then he was a giant. But a benevolent one. I came up to the bottom of his fly when I was first included in more serious sessions on the court. It wasn't until a further four years had passed that I could look the zipper in the eye.

Armed only with the family bat that dragged awkwardly behind my steps to the crease, I would struggle for perfect backlift. It was too big for me. It was my brother's bat. It had to be swung surely. What is now an instinctive habit was then a determined effort as its weight tugged at my developing forearms.

Once momentum was achieved it was difficult to stop mid-shot. Many times I cursed inwardly as the path of the departing ball flew a gentle arc into the waiting hands of the most disinterested fielder.

Father recognised my problem and altered the rules to compensate for my immature limbs. Yet he too appeared a Goliath, carefully positioned in front of the setting sun, relishing the conditions of bounce and turn with the contented smile of one who knows he is about to secure a wicket.

The enduring impression of that silhouette is of height combined with legendary leanness of Coney form. Father Mantis. A man who needed three sets of shin pads to cover knee to ankle. He played all parts: bowler, fielder, umpire, and threatened continually to become a commentator. Every shot was followed by encouragement or warning.

Generally his comments bordered on profound pessimism and the strategy the bowler should employ to expose the pretender. Each batsman was another challenge, another opportunity to reveal his skill. He always took special pleasure in beating the bat with his unique armoury — the high looping slower ball which when it pitched, spun viciously towards the groin; the quicker 'shin-crusher' that caused chronic bruising to my front leg, and the unsettling 'beamer' that would plunge me headlong onto the cold hard asphalt.

Father's enthusiasm was all-consuming. His raucous appeals for catches behind or lbw often upset neighbours' cats in season, and caused our clematis to become barren the following spring. Under his guidance I learned the basics of playing forward and back, to move the feet, to lean the shoulder, to roll the wrists. He never played cricket himself, yet his devotion was that curious mixture of the aesthetic and the obsessive. We had a routine. Dad would return home, drape his paisley dressing gown on his spare frame and tune up. The violin sat ready and waiting. And as the strains of Beethoven wafted on Wellington air I warmed up myself with a backyard adaptation for single players.

It involved a sacrifice by Mother. In pre-television days when a bout of after-school loneliness struck, I headed for Mother's top drawer. It housed her stockings — the gossamer mesh type so ideally suited to test matches. A cricket ball could be inserted, and in no time at all could hang suspended from the clothesline. I was lucky my mother was tall. With the combined weight of the ball and the length of the foreleg, it rotated tantalisingly at forward defence height. It was a simple game. There were two sides of international repute. I made myself captain and opening bat, in fact I was the entire batting side. The stocking swung freely when struck with the stump I was given by Uncle Morris. I would watch its return closely and attempt to hit it again and add a further run to the total. A miss meant a wicket had fallen.

The weather played a crucial part in this game. First the wind tended to blow the ball and change its swing dramatically. Secondly, if it was fine, the weight of other clothes on the line encouraged the knot to loosen and periodically slip towards the sheets. This demanded nimble feet, not only to readjust to the wicket a yard to the right, but also to avoid being enveloped by wildly flapping linen.

It was a game I enjoyed immensely, despite words from Mother about the rapid deterioration of her latest silks. These solitary innings filled my afternoons and often the twilight hours of my childhood. Through them I began the process of reading the line, waiting until the last second to play. They were good for self esteem because there was never a chance of a witnessed failure. The failures were private, and your overwhelming desire to succeed in the company of test heroes was assured.

Jeremy Coney *The Playing Mantis* (1985)

For those not lucky enough to come from a cricketing family, there are other ways to learn the game. Clarrie Grimmett's introduction came from the cricket-mad Harris boys who lived next door, and he honed the skills he would later use to become one of the world's legendary spin bowlers under the eagle eye of the sportsmaster at Wellington's Mount Cook Boys' School.

Clarrie was aged six when he began to follow the older Harris kids as they tripped happily down to Wellington's famous Basin Reserve to have a hit. George Harris was fifteen, Charles, ten and Arthur, eight. The boys would play impromptu cricket matches in the street, with an asphalt pitch and a telegraph pole for stumps. The flint-hard track proved a true surface. It provided bounce and ample breadth of turn. These cricket–mad urchins of Wellington would scatter in all directions at the sudden appearance of uniformed Constable Thirsk, who would seem to materialise out of the gloom. He was huge. A good–natured fellow, he was never able to win the boys' confidence. They were too busy hiding.

He was a cartoonist's dream. *Punch* would be proud to promote him in its well-read pages. Constable Thirsk would give a little chuckle to himself and hurriedly leave the scene, for he knew the light was fading fast. There could be time for five more overs. He duly noted the arms and legs protruding at odd and ungainly angles from behind the roadside hedge. However, he also knew that there was danger for the boys at dusk, though traffic was not the hectic stream of today when Clarrie was a boy. There were no motor vehicles, but a bolting horse, with a dray in tow, presented real danger to any child in its path.

The cricket was of the spartan kind: no gloves or pads (Clarrie would later learn that his hero, Victor Trumper, preferred not to wear batting gloves). The inevitable bruise was worn with pride — a battle scar; the painful reminder of combat. Players simply had to watch the ball all the way, and miss it at their own peril! Cricket was very much a labour of love for Clarrie, who always tried to emulate his hero Trumper. He would charge down the track to a Harris leg-break and smite it with all his power, imagining that he was the great Victor Trumper, who had advanced down the wicket with quick and sure footwork to meet the Bosanquet delivery and caress the half-volley to the mid-off boundary. The crowd erupted! Trumper settled down once more — then Clarrie was brought back to earth with a resounding thump, as a Harris leg-break clean-bowled him and almost simultaneously Mary Grimmett declared: 'Clarrie! Dinner's on the table!'

Mary and Richard Grimmett gave Clarrie plenty of love and encouragement; however, they knew little of the game. They always provided their son with creams and the equipment he needed to give of his best. They applauded his successes and helped to ease the hurt of failure.

The Basin Reserve became a sort of Mecca for Clarrie and the Harris boys. Most of the Basin Reserve was in excellent order in those days, a few years before the Boer War and Trumper's triumphant tour of England in 1902. However, a portion of this famous ground was rather neglected. As rough as any Australian cow paddock, this was the area open for use by anyone — usually most of the kids in the neighbourhood. Often Clarrie was the one entrusted to carry the spade George Harris (junior) would use to smooth out the rough spots on their pitch. It was an unwritten law: first in, first served. The youngsters had to get to the ground early to grab the best batting strip. The very idea of having to use a spade to help 'smooth' the wicket indicates that the pitches must have been particularly helpful to the fielding team. All the boys loved to bowl out of the back of the hand and their well-spun offerings rewarded them with exaggerated turn on those uneven surfaces. Clarrie's expertise in bowling leg-breaks greatly impressed the Harris brothers. He needed to be good to keep up with his older spin mates, for all the Harris boys could make the ball curve in flight, turn and bounce.

Ever the small one, Clarrie's very name seemed to suit him. He was slight, but wiry and seemingly tireless. He revelled in not merely dismissing a batsman, but in making the ball fizz, spinning it in such a controlled and calculated manner that it often humbled his opponent. He enjoyed the ecstasy of bowling. He toiled to deceive. From the early days, Clarrie found that it was the combination of flight and breadth of turn that would defeat a batsman. It was not good enough simply to turn the ball, nor was it sufficient to toss it up without spinning hard. He tried that method and found that the only scientific reason for the ball to fall to earth was gravity. He decided to give gravity a helping hand. By spinning the ball hard and over the top, Clarrie found that the ball dipped; the harder he spun it, the more acute was the dip. It also would make a humming sound. The sound of that humming ball heralded the demise of many a fine batsman; the victim's funeral march was music to Clarrie's ears.

The humming song of spin, however, was not the real danger for batsmen. It was the imparted over-spin which caused the ball to dip and land slightly shorter than the batsman calculated. This deceived him in flight. Clarrie realised the importance of the position of the wrist and how the wrist position could dictate the various angles of turn. The more over-spin the bowler gained, the more dip and bounce; the less over-spin, or bowling the leg-break with the seam 'square on' to the batsman, the greater the breadth of turn, the slighter the bounce.

Clarrie began to study and question why a ball behaved in a particular way. Not yet in his teens, Clarrie developed an investigative curiosity. He found that commonsense must prevail. There was always an explanation for the manner in which a ball, held in a certain way, would react in relation to the forces applied to it. His approach to cricket was never clouded by theory. Spin always held its fascination. It served Clarrie well in those encounters with and against the Harris brothers.

Yet when it came to the all-important showpiece, school cricket, Clarrie was not entirely convinced about the value of spin bowling. In those games, Clarrie rushed in and bowled as fast as he could. Any ball bowled at a pace less than flat out and he reckoned it would invite heavy and severe punishment. Spin bowling was the thing furthest from Clarrie's mind when he ran in to bowl at the Mount Cook Boys' School nets. At the age of fourteen, Clarrie was so slight that he could have passed for a boy much younger. He was, however, strong and wiry and he could bowl at a remarkable speed. Good judges in junior cricket had already marked Grimmett down as likely to develop into a fine fast bowler. There was one proviso. Clarrie would need to fill out and grow. But Clarrie never did grow very tall, nor did he become very robust. He remained spare, but he lacked neither resolve nor stamina. Mount Cook Boys' School nets became the place to learn the art of cricket.

The school sportsmaster, F.A. 'Dimp' Hempelmann, was something of a demon to the boys. They admired and respected him, for his love of sport was evident. More importantly, he cared for his young charges. He was tough, but fair. Under Hempelmann's keen eye it was general practice for each of the bowlers to finish their stint in the nets by bowling six balls in succession. Hempelmann was wise enough to know that great effort was required to finish the session in this manner. He watched intently. This was the test of character. There was never a harsh word. Hempelmann had the knack of putting a boy in his place by raising his eyebrows. This rebuff would follow a long-hop or a similar poor delivery. The boys expected it, just as they rejected any praise for anything less than a stroke right out of the top drawer or a brilliant delivery. False praise was a rare commodity at Mount Cook.

One afternoon, Clarrie was letting fly with his six quick deliveries. He put every effort into his work, but by the end of the over, after a heavy workload on that warm day, Clarrie was nearly spent. Hempelmann observed Grimmett's six deliveries. He was impressed, but not quite satisfied.

'Clarrie, would you please send me down another six balls?' he asked.

Young Grimmett could hardly stand, let alone rush in and bowl again. Wearily he meandered back to his mark, careful to take his normal full run, and began his approach.

The boys had been bowling for a good hour before Hempelmann called for the final six deliveries. Now Clarrie was being called upon to bowl yet another six balls. He was exhausted. Another six balls? The request might just as well have been to run up to the top of Mount Cook wearing army boots. Despite all his efforts to maintain a good rhythm, Clarrie stumbled up to the wicket. Lost to fatigue, his usual rhythm deserted him. He felt limp and lethargic, at the point of collapse. It may have been a combination of fatigue and mischief in Clarrie which caused him suddenly to grip the ball differently and send down what the Harris brothers already knew to be Grimmett's special and most gifted trademark — a perfectly pitched leg-break.

The ball curved in slightly and upon pitching, it gripped on the responsive, soft and yielding turf and spun prodigiously across the unsuspecting batsman.

He missed the ball by a mile and Hempelmann could hardly contain his glee.

'Ah, Mr Grimmett, that is better. From now on, my young man, you shall bowl only leg-breaks. Yes, Mr Grimmett, it is leg-breaks from now on.'

Ashley Mallet *Clarrie Grimmett: The Bradman of Spin* (1993)

Perhaps obsession is the hallmark of the great player. Grimmett was for ever experimenting, whether he had a cricket ball to hand or not. As the Australian cricket writer, Ray Robinson, put it: 'When he took an orange at dinner it must have required all his self-control not to make it circle round the cruet and bowl the celery, middle stump.' The young Glenn Turner, locked in pavement combat with his brother Brian, showed the same determined temperament. He learned how to calculate the shots that brought the best results, and would have liked to bat for ever.

There was a long, narrow alleyway between our house and the one next door. The gap was wide of mid-on. If you could guide the ball down the alley you could just about run four before the fieldsman was able to get to it and return. If you hit the ball elsewhere in the yard there was only time to run a single. But down the alley was different. The fieldsman couldn't return the ball to the wicket from down there, he had to run all the way back to the yard with the ball before he could get the necessary arm-room to throw it back. If Brian or I chased it there'd be only three runs in it; with any of the others you might make four.

I made a point of trying to hit the ball down that alley as often as I could and I think this is one of the main reasons why, earlier in my career, I was stronger through mid-on, or certainly through the on side, than I was on the off.

If we weren't playing back-yard cricket we'd be out on the footpath with the ashcan or a butter box as a wicket. We played a lot of this sort of cricket a few years later when we were living in South Dunedin. Brian would come home from net practice with the first eleven and outside we'd go until dark. If I won the toss I'd bat all night if I could, until it became so dark we'd have to stop; and then the next night I'd insist on starting where I'd left off. We played with a tennis ball on a pitch of about sixteen or seventeen yards. The tennis ball would swing a bit, but with mostly only the two of us playing, the bowler having to field his own bowling, and lbw's almost impossible to agree on, it was difficult to get someone out. If you could drive the ball back past the bowler so that it missed all the parked cars and ran almost to the end of the block, then this was really rubbing it in to the poor bowler who had to retrieve it himself. Brian would sometimes throw his wicket away if he wanted a bowl. I never would; I knew I'd get a bowl sometime; I wanted to bat.

Glenn Turner *My Way* (1975)

Even for those who acquire the cricketing habit early, there is sometimes a blinding moment of revelation that transforms interest into passion.

On a mad March day in 1933, Walter Hammond broke the world test Match record by scoring 336 not out against New Zealand bowlers who could not do much more than admire the regal power of his stroke-making. Hammond in that innings hit ten sixes. One of them, I recall, landed only inches from a gentleman who had taken liberal steps to console himself against the prospect of a New Zealand defeat, and who dozed quietly on the terrace. No doubt he is still telling his grandchildren about the magnificence of Hammond's batting.

Three of Hammond's sixes came from successive balls from the Nelson slow left-hander, Jack Newman (later to become a New Zealand selector) and were majestic on-drives just wide of the sightscreen. I was one of a pack of boys scrambling and fighting to retrieve the ball after it had fallen behind us. Once I won possession, and earned the distinction of being able to throw it back to a fieldsman who probably wished he could offer the bowler a hand-grenade. It certainly did not occur to me that I too, would play test cricket one day or that I would be the fieldsman to take the catch that would end Hammond's great test career. This happened at Christchurch in 1947.

I believe it was that memorable display by one of England's greatest batsmen that kindled the spark of ambition in me. I suppose something similar has happened thousands of times in hundreds of places — a great batsman or bowler is watched by a youngster with an interest in cricket, but who sees, for the first time, the real beauty and fascination of the summer game.

Bert Sutcliffe *Between Overs* (1963)

Can you learn anything about playing cricket from books? I once saved my pocket money to buy a small, green-covered volume called *How to Score a Century*. It was full of line drawings showing batsmen executing impossibly perfect shots with nonchalant ease. For months, I sneaked into my parents' bedroom, book in one hand, bat in the other, to practise in front of the dressing-table mirror. The power of books on impressionable cricketing minds should not be underestimated!

The night before our game at the Hutt Rec against Otago, Brian Cederwall began reading a book that would change his life. For almost 48 hours. It was *Allan Davidson's Cricket Book of Bowling for Boys*, which purported to show how different grips could make the ball do just about anything. Cedes was inspired. This would turn him into a great bowler, just like Davo.

The stage was set. Now, since it was a bitterly cold day, no-one was in a hurry to bowl into the howling northerly. No-one except Cedes, that is, and it wasn't long before he took his first wicket. He rushed down the track screaming, 'It worked, it worked!' 'What worked?' said someone. It was then that he revealed the first of his new techniques. This was to run up behind the umpire and suddenly appear so that the batsman couldn't see him in time. He alleged it was from Davo's book.

His confidence grew. He began to experiment. He varied the pace of his run up by sprinting the first few steps, jogging the next, back to sprinting, then back to jogging, before sprinting from behind the umpire to deliver the ball. I believe there may have been a slight misunderstanding. I'm sure Davo meant vary the pace of the delivery. But it didn't really matter because Cedes soon took another wicket.

It was, he claimed the result of one of Davo's grips which he described in detail. He was urging all of us to read *Allan Davidson's Cricket Book of Bowling for Boys*. Something one or two were tempted to do after he'd bowled the next ball. Putting his fingernails into the seam he ran/jogged up, bowled, the ball which pitched on a good length then went along the ground and hit the base of the stumps. The stunned silence was broken by the scream of 'Sustanooda!' from Cedes. A sustanooda, he explained, was the name he'd chosen for this particular Davo speciality.

By now, he was getting completely carried away. He started to try to do everything in one ball. Varying the pace, running behind the umpire with his fast/slow/fast/slow/fast momentum, side stepping and then bowling by incorporating several different grips as well as variations in his arm action. Eventually he delivered another sustanooda. He was beside himself. 'Davo, you're brilliant,' he said to no-one in particular. By this stage, the rest of the team had had enough. We asked him if he'd considered the state of the pitch. 'No mate,' he replied. 'It's Davo. Davo's doing it for me.' Unfortunately, his illusions were shattered the following day when it was our turn to bat. The bowler at Cedes end had a field day, including one or two sustanoodas. And he swore blind he'd never even heard of *Allan Davidson's Cricket Book of Bowling for Boys*.

Bruce Edgar with David Roberts **Bruce Edgar: An Opener's Tale** (1987)

Active participation in cricket often ends on leaving school. By then, those with more talent, or greater determination, have probably already embarked on the next stage of learning the game by joining a proper club.

 Club loyalties run deep. As a child I lived Saturday morning competition with Onslow Cricket Club.

It was a natural progression to join their ranks after college. Indeed, during the holidays between anxious phone calls to girls and adolescent acne, I was occasionally drafted into lower grade teams. Here I learned to cope with the extra speed and bounce of artful, mature bowlers, assisted by irregular virgin club wickets.

I met the subtleties of Indian Sporting Club spinners and the captivating enthusiasm of Pacific Islanders hell-bent on putting the first cricket ball on the moon. I always had trouble with spinners even though they gave me more time to see it. They usually got me out, my downfall always an act of unrestrained impetuosity. I was completely in until I was returning just beyond the boundary, suddenly disconsolately out.

After the fast bowlers were swept aside, an Indian spinner stepped up to the bowling crease. They set his field and he prepared to bowl. It took some time to arrive. As my mind calculated its path I took bold steps out of the crease to meet it as it fell, the bat pressed powerfully forward to give its own greeting to this new challenge. There was a stifled cry from the slip area and the keeper cursed in Punjabi doggerel. He should have completed an easy stumping with me still shaking hands with the non-striker.

After the next delivery I picked myself up from the crease and searched in vain for comfort. My tormentor turned away unconcerned with the earth-shattering havoc he was causing in my life. I clung to well-meaning phrases given by a variety of sources. And so as my Nemesis trotted in all in the same moment I tried to get to the pitch and smother it, as Father advised, to hit him off his length, as my team-mate suggested, push for a single, as the coaching manual recommended and pad up which was my natural inclination. These alternatives left me in a tangle on the ground. I was stumped or bowled. Suddenly those commentators who spoke of Iverson and Ramadhin began to make sense and I examined myself in a hitherto different light. This man had my measure and was toying with me. The cane pads filled with lead, my boots took root and my bat became that curious mixture of too heavy and too small. I determined I must ask for greater variety from Father's sessions.

The Pacific Islanders were quite different. Their approach was easy to see. Every bowler had to rival Harold Larwood's speed off three paces, every ball had to be despatched over the boundary. I'm sure Ian Botham and Lance Cairns lived with this race when they were boys.

Our fielding usually wilted under the pressure. Grown men broke into tears when asked to field on the on-side so the captain had to do it. I well remember Don Baker, a lovely man, circling underneath one at short mid-wicket, holding a lengthy discussion with the keeper, while the ball was still rising, about whose responsibility it was to get under the high ball. The keeper dismissed this plea because he hadn't paid up his personal insurance premiums.

There were some wonderful dismissals. Bats ending up at square leg, wickets beaten to the ground, ludicrous run-outs because both batsmen wanted to see what happened when the ball fell, each downfall met with uproarious laughter from batsmen and team-mates from the boundary.

Later, back in the safety of the club rooms, we dissected our performance in the true spirit of the game, chatting over a beer, forming lasting friendships. Paul Neal, who despite good intentions, still can't play straight more than an over. Terry O'Reilly, who played a mean piano. Graham Lark, expert of the tennis indoor ball game. Club stalwarts Jim Linton and Ken Lines and so many more. Against this accepting yet competitive backdrop I grew to learn and develop the skills.

Jeremy Coney *The Playing Mantis* (1985)

Playing cricket sometimes seems a little like musical chairs — or maybe Russian roulette. At each level of the game more and more players drop out, until only a very few are left. The number of club cricketers who go on to play for their province is small. Once upon a time, before the present-day obsession with Youth, Academy and other sorts of hybrid elevens, those who became provincial representatives were rewarded by having the chance to play against touring international sides. As sports journalist Spiro Zavos recalls, the contest may have been unequal but the occasion was one to remember for life.

Throughout my cricket career I had a problem, one of many, which captains never seemed able to resolve. No one could work out whether I was an ordinary, competent opening bat, a number one, or a very good last man in, a number 11. Cricket terminology, for those ignorant of its arcane truths, works on the opposite scale of the Bo Derek mode.

From season to season, and sometimes from match to match, I would find myself either a cricketing one (the equivalent of the Bo Derek 10) or a number 11 (the equivalent of a one). It made things confusing for opponents but doubly confusing for me. I believed I had cricket's first identity crisis.

When the representative season started in 1958 I was selected in a Wellington B team to tour the Hawke's Bay area. The first game of the tour found me at number 11. There were the delights of buxom hotel room cleaners to provide some consolation for this drop in the batting order. I fell in love with one very cuddly young woman in Dannevirke, bought her copies of the latest hit single, 'Tom Dooley', by the Kingston Trio. The one-sided romance ended as quickly as it began when I went to the toilet in the middle of the night and discovered her creeping out of the room of one of the more senior members of our team.

Nothing concentrates the mind like a heart believed to be shattered. For the rest of the tour dalliance was put aside. By the last crucial match, against a strong Wanganui side, I had been promoted to opener.

I made a fluent 40 or so in the first innings before trying to hit a spinner out of the ground, only to be stumped. We needed about 150 runs in the second innings in a great hurry to win the game. To the surprise of everyone, including myself, I tore the bowling apart. When my partner had scored about three or four runs, I was racing towards a 50. On the strength of an electrifying start, we won the match comfortably. At the conclusion of the tour, our manager, Diddy Knapp, a cagey veteran, nominated me as player of the tour, expressing surprise at the quality of my batting.

The Wellington representative 11 meanwhile had performed poorly in the Plunket Shield matches. Two more games were left for something to be salvaged from the ruined season — a one-day match against a side selected by Lord Cobham, the Governor-General, to be followed the next weekend by a three-day match against a full-strength England team that had just finished playing a test series in Australia.

There was not much surprise in the press, or among the players, when the selectors named several youngsters, including myself, for these two matches.

The Governor-General got perfect weather for his match. We won the toss and on the stroke of 11, before a crowd of thousands all expectant of a day's high entertainment, I made my way to the wicket with another youngster, Jim Morison, to face the opening over from the legendary Australian fast bowler and batsman Keith Miller.

It's impossible to play any sport seriously without developing little superstitions. One of mine was that if I opened, I had to take the first ball. I had reasoned that statistically it was most unlikely that the first few balls of a match would result in a wicket falling. As I had failed maths comprehensively in School Certificate, I think my reasoning was a trifle wobbly. Nevertheless, as we made our way out to the wicket, my offer to take the first ball was accepted with what might be described as alacrity by my nervous batting partner.

So there I was, a batsman of dubious quality, who had never faced a really fast bowler in his life, watching the characteristically bustling run-up of Keith Miller to the wicket. It was a run-up I was totally familiar with. I had seen it many times demonstrated on films, with the end result a bouncer whistling past the astonished eyebrows of some England batsman, or a stump being catapulted out of the sockets.

And there were all those marvellous photos of Miller, black hair streaming in the wind, body poised in a classic frieze before sending down another searing delivery. Although the great bowler had been retired for four years, he had finished his test career on a high note, capturing 10 wickets for the match in one of his last bowling onslaughts. And his victims then were among the all-time greats of cricket, people like Sir Len Hutton and Denis Compton.

And now he was bowling to me.

Whizz!!! The first ball was past before I had time to move the bat. As it whirled on its venomous way to the wicketkeeper it nicked my shirt collar. Another inch lower and a broken shoulder may have resulted.

The great man raced in again. I tried to shut out the noise of the crowd, but this was impossible, I had the sort of feeling that the Christians being fed to the lions must have experienced — of being surrounded by thousands of voyeurs who are not really interested in whether you survive, but intent instead on seeing blood flow and the action and drama proceed unchecked.

This time it was another bouncer. But I was ready for it. I swatted it away to the boundary. There was a roar like the surging of a great ocean. The Christian striking back had turned the crowd, for this instant anyway, to my side. Several more bouncers followed which I evaded easily enough. These were the days before helmets so most players were more experienced about ensuring they were not hit on the head than they are now.

One thing I noticed about those balls I could see was that although Miller was bowling at a high pace he was still able to move the ball about, especially away from the bat (the most dangerous ball in the game), far more than bowlers of less pace I had faced. Scientists have calculated that the faster a ball is bowled, the less likely it is to swing. The greatness of Miller's bowling, I suppose, was that the laws of nature which applied to ordinary mortals appeared to be suspended in his case.

The other aspect of his bowling that intrigued me was its great variety. The amount of swing varied from ball to ball. The bouncer was fired down with exactly the same action as for a fuller-pitched ball. Batsmen are like boxers and watching the feet and arm action can give a good indication of what sort of ball is likely to come down: boxers rarely concentrate on their opponent's gloves and, in the same way, a batsman who is concerned with watching the ball to the exclusion of other indicators will not last long at the crease. By having the same action for all his different deliveries, Miller was, as cricketers say, 'difficult to read'.

Towards the end of his bowling stint, Miller raced in and, without telegraphing what he was going to do, bowled me a beautifully controlled leg-spinner. I smacked it away to the boundary. But as the applause died I realised that the humour and skill of the delivery deserved a less belligerent reply. I felt like a boy who had stamped on a butterfly just because it was within reach.

When we gathered in the dressing room before taking the field to bowl to Lord Cobham's team, Bob Vance, our captain, gave us some instructions: 'For God's sake, don't bowl, catch or run out Miller before he's scored a few runs. The crowd's come to see him bat, not us bowl or field. If he hits a catch, try to drop it without making it too obvious.' With that set of warnings ringing in our ears, we made our way out into the sunlight.

At the fall of the first wicket, the great man strode in to bat. I was fielding on a distant boundary and had a feeling of sorrow for him. The poor fellow was likely to give a chance early on in the piece. He would have to be nurtured through the difficult early minutes of his innings.

I had taken Bob Vance's warnings too much to heart. Miller flayed our bowling. Even to the medium-pacers he was yards down the pitch, whacking the ball to every part of the ground. From my position on the boundary I was able to enjoy the spectacle. My main task was to retrieve the ball from spectators whose lives had been endangered as it descended upon them.

After Miller had taken about 70 runs from us in as many minutes, I innocently asked our captain whether we could catch him now. This being a family magazine, the reply perhaps should not be printed.

It was with a sense of foreboding and a deep awareness of my fallibility as a player that I walked out, with the other players in the Wellington side, to try to dismiss the England team.

For most of the day, we emulated the birds in the fields who, the Bible tells us, 'neither sowed nor spun'. The England batsmen piled on the runs. They were several classes too good for us. Our main bowler was the speedster Bob Blair. There never has been a bowler more feared in his own country than Blair. He did not just dismiss batsmen, he sent them to hospital (especially Canterbury batsmen). The mere presence of Blair intimidated New Zealand batsmen. I accepted this general sense of awe as I had several times faced him without success.

However, when the elegant Tom Graveney was batting, I was given an insight into how lacking in real class Bob Blair was. I was at mid-on when Blair bowled a bouncer to Graveney. The ball scudded instead of rising and the batsman had to dig down quickly to scoop it away to the boundary. As he jogged down the pitch, he called out to Blair: 'Bob, try and get those bouncers to get up a bit, can't you?'

This is the ultimate insult to a fast bowler. Blair stood at the wicket demanding the ball. 'Give me the bloody thing,' he called out, 'I'm going to knock his bloody head off.'

Watching from close quarters, I felt sorry for Graveney and the wrath that was about to descend upon him. Blair came storming in. He made a galvanic leap and with a huge grunt released a steepling bouncer that rose like a rocket straight for the batsman's throat. Graveney calmly leant back and flicked the ball, as if it were a fly on his sleeve, away to the boundary. He jogged down the pitch as a fieldsman scurried after the ball. 'Just put them there, Bob, that's really perfect.'

Those words and the action that had preceded them convinced me that I was out of my league.

Soon enough, the next morning, after 400 or so runs had been scored against us, it was our turn to bat. The contest between David and Goliath was about to be repeated, with the giant certain to win.

As was my habit, I took the first ball from Freddie Trueman. I had met him at a parliamentary reception several days earlier. The great man had been dragged away from a conversation with the Prime Minister to be photographed with me. He held a cup in his bowling grip with me looking up to him with wonder and admiration: 'Master shows pupil his grip,' the caption to the photo read. What I remembered most about the encounter was Trueman's bulk; he was a burly man with a vast bottom. He was brusque. And he wore blue suede shoes with a brown suit. None of this, I told myself, as I tossed and turned the night before I had to bat, augured well for me.

There I was, strangely calm, despite everything, while in the near distance Trueman began his long, thundering run to the wickets. It was the longest run-up I had ever experienced. My concentration went off and on the boil several times as he pounded in. Then there was a leap at the wicket, the flashing arm, a red fuzz of a ball hurtling towards me and the bowler himself charging down the pitch on his follow-through like a runaway locomotive, all dark, threatening and steamed-up.

I jabbed my bat down. The ball squirted away to leg. Two runs. The crowd erupted into applause. The bowler came down the pitch and in blue Yorkshire argot berated the fieldsman who had missed the ball. Trueman then marched back to his mark somewhere near the sightscreen, every now and then stopping to turn and cast dark, baleful glares towards me and the unhappy fieldsman.

In the agonising moments in which all this took place, I remembered our captain's instructions to take my bat up before the bowler let the ball go because 'you won't have time to take it up and bring it down with someone of Trueman's pace'. Also there was the scene in the dressing room with the older and more experienced players donning all sorts of chest and thigh pads as protectors. As I slipped my small pink box into place and put on the schoolboy pads I liked to bat in, I was visited with the sort of looks that I imagined a man going out to the electric chair is given from his fellow prisoners.

The protection proved totally inadequate, anyway, when the next ball ripped into my thigh, only inches away from putting my box to the ultimate test. I collapsed to the ground, weakened by pain and fear. The crowd roared. Players gathered around me wanting to know if I was all right, where did it hit, vital parts all right — that sort of thing.

Strangely, after that, I was right. I began to play Trueman, not exactly confidently; he was too good for me (or anyone at the time) to do that. But I was middling the ball. I found I could pick the bouncer by seeing whether his shoulder dipped markedly at the moment of delivery. The crowd loved it as I threw myself to the ground to avoid the rearing ball.

Frank Tyson, who was no longer the force he was four years earlier when he was rated the fastest bowler in the history of the game, I found more difficult. Trueman moved the ball away from the batsman. On several occasions, I was, as the saying goes, 'not good enough' to get a touch. Tyson, a great pace, cut the ball into the batsman. The ball was forever threatening my chest or if it were a bit lower, my little pinkie.

Bereft of wickets in Australia, he was determined to make amends in New Zealand. Hefty grunts preceded balls of awesome pace. When he pitched one ball short, I think in my second innings, I leant back and with a legitimate square cut crashed it to the boundary. In the hundreds of hours I had played cricket, that particular moment was probably the zenith of my performances.

I had settled in so well, however, that a school friend, who had travelled down from Auckland on the night train to see me play, decided to sneak out of the ground before lunch to get some fish and chips before the crowd invaded the shop. As he was making his way back to the ground, he heard a great roar. He got inside the ground just in time to see my little figure wending in melancholy fashion back to the pavilion.

What he hadn't seen (nor had I for that matter) was a particularly fast ball from Tyson that was on me before I could give it the full blade of the bat. It flew off the edge straight to Ted Dexter in the slips who snaffled it with the ease of a magician with a handkerchief.

It was the sheer persistency of pace, from both ends, that finally undid me. I knew that I could keep any individual ball out. But sooner or later the continual sequence of fast balls was certain to find out my deficiencies. It was no consolation that, except for my fellow opener Bruce Murray (later to play for New Zealand) and Bob Vance (a cultured 50), everyone else was unsuccessful. The gap between our inexperience and dreams and the reality of great professional players was too much.

The next season I was put back to number 11. My form and interest degenerated and I faded out of the game. At parties, one of my less tactful friends took to introducing me as 'the only player in the world over the hill at 21'.

Spiro Zavos 'Facing the Giants', *New Zealand Listener* 3 March 1984

Playing for your province must be the peak of many cricketers' ambitions. This is where reality sets in, the time when work commitments, career prospects, personal responsibilities and lack of finance, have to be weighed against an unpredictable future. Can you go on to further honours, or will you be one of those who are never quite good enough to take the next step up the cricketing ladder? For provincial players to know that they are in the New Zealand selectors' minds must be tremendously reassuring — even when that knowledge comes at a cost...

I'll never forget the day in 1978 when I got the Big Phone Call. I think it was on a Wednesday. Perhaps it was Thursday. It was from the president of the Central Districts Cricket Association. Or maybe it was someone else. It certainly wasn't anyone from the New Zealand Cricket Council selection committee.

I was asked to go to Napier and be substitute fielder in the second test against Pakistan. The twelfth man was Jumbo Anderson and I don't know if it was NZCC policy in those days to send the twelfth man home or it was punishment for Jumbo dropping Miandad in the first test when he was on nought. In any case, they needed someone else in the field. So they chose me.

I threw my gear bag in the back of my old 1968 red Hillman Hunter and as I drove through the Manawatu Gorge towards sunny Hawke's Bay, I was buzzing with excitement.

On arriving at Napier I found that the NZCC would not pay for me to actually stay in the hotel with the team. I was put up instead at the home of David O'Sullivan, the former Central Districts and New Zealand spinner. But it didn't matter. I was where I wanted to be, where I always wanted to be, inside the New Zealand dressing room.

Apart from a few controversial umpiring decisions and Hadlee getting his hundredth test wicket, the game was dominated by rain and ended in a disappointing draw. I doubt that anyone would even remember I was there. I did manage to get on the field a couple of times and while I didn't do anything spectacular like taking a catch, I did my best to run hard and look impressive.

Finally, when it was all over and the New Zealand team packed up to fly to Auckland for the third and final test, I packed up to head back to Palmerston North and my job at the bank.

But before I left, the manager and chief selector of the New Zealand team, Frank Cameron, strolled over and gave me $100 for my trouble. I was absolutely staggered. I had played, be it as substitute, for New Zealand, I'd had a taste of the big time. I had been able to watch players prepare for a test innings. I had watched bowlers prepare for a bowling spell. I had been able to watch Wally Lees prepare for another day's wicketkeeping. And on top of that I had $100 in my pocket!

Life was rich!

I was on top of the world as I drove back towards the Manawatu. Well, I was until the car broke down. The Hillman just conked out on the side of the road, halfway through the gorge. Of all the stretches of road in New Zealand to break down, this was one of the worst!

No problem though. I hitched a ride to the next service station and arranged for them to tow the car to their garage and fix it for me. It was a simple enough job. Just the alternator needed replacing.

Then came the bad news. They wanted $99.95 for the tow and the replacement part. I found myself reaching into my back pocket and withdrawing the wonderful $100 note I had been given just three hours before and handing it to the mechanic.

He handed me back the change. I looked at it incredulously. I couldn't believe it. There it was, the result of my first experience of professional cricket. After expenses, five cents. Five cents for five days' cricket? One cent a day.

Ian Smith, as told to Roger Brittenden *Smithy: Just a Drummer in the Band* (1991)

The financial rewards for playing test cricket have become a great deal better since then, but all cricketing autobiographies confirm that playing for your country is not primarily a matter of money. For many cricketers, hearing their name read out in a test team for the first time is one of the most emotional occasions of a lifetime.

'K.R. Rutherford,' I heard. My mind, my body was numb. I had set this goal for myself for as long as I could remember. Suddenly I had achieved it. At 19 I was in the same team as Richard Hadlee, Jeremy Coney, Ian Smith, John Wright and all the names I'd imagined playing alongside for my country. As people congratulated me I couldn't find a reply. I had no idea how to react. Warren Lees, with whom I'd played senior cricket since I was 15 and who'd been such a positive force in Otago cricket, then pulled me aside. 'This is the most important thing you've achieved in your life,' he said. Some form of realisation then slowly sunk in and emotion began to overwhelm me. I went out to a balcony and looked across the Basin Reserve and said slowly to myself over and over 'I'm going to play for New Zealand.' As I stood there, on my own, I began to cry uncontrollably.

Ken Rutherford and Chris Mirams *A Hell of a Way to Make a Living* (1995)

Is cricket a game that can ever be mastered completely? Commentators, many of them former test players, say that the gulf between provincial and test cricket is enormous. Being picked for New Zealand is just the start of another learning process. Cricket is a sport that can make fools of the most accomplished and has a cruel way of demolishing long-cherished ambitions. For years the great J.R. Reid dreamed of playing in a test match for New Zealand at Lord's — but when he first did so, he found that he still had a lot to learn about the game...

Lord's...
J.R. Reid, b. Bailey 0.

There it was, the death-knell of my boyhood ambitions — my first innings at Lord's...Lord's with its hallowed shrine atmosphere...the tummy butterflies fluttering madly as I wait to go to the crease...Trevor Bailey moving in with that alert, cocked-head, almost lop-sided action of his — running in to bowl to me.

This is it. Here I am at Lord's, an England bowler about to deliver to the twenty-year-old fledgling of the 1949 New Zealand team's nest.

Over it comes.

Glory be, it's a half-volley. It's hittable on the drive.

But do I drive? Do I unfold the classic stroke so long reserved for this very moment, the first ball of my first innings at Lord's? The one which would have the members applauding with unrestrained delight?

Do I? As an old friend of mine used to say, 'In a pig's eye I do.'

I play back to this juicy half-volley and I'm gone, gone, gone. I hear the woody rattle in an agony of despair and silent self-condemnation.

Lord's — the W.G. Grace Gates, the Long Room…

Lord's — the glass-encased relics, the crooked bats, the bird killed in startled flight by a cruelly vagrant ball…

Lord's — the picture of Bradman…

Lord's — and I have made a blodger!

J.R. Reid *Sword of Willow* (1962)

AMONG THE IMMORTALS

Tom Lowry, that combative batsman of the 1920s and '30s, once declared that the five best cricketers this country had produced were Dan Reese, Sid Hiddleston, Martin Donnelly, Bert Sutcliffe and Jack Cowie. Writing in 1986, one of New Zealand's finest sports journalists, T.P. McLean, chose as his five Dempster, Sutcliffe, Cowie, Glenn Turner and Richard Hadlee. The urge to pick the greatest — either of your own day or of all time — is as irresistible to cricketers and sportswriters as it is to cricket lovers. Almost every follower of the game has a view on the matter.

It is true that cricketing exploits can be summarised in coldly impersonal statistics, but these cannot evaluate a performance. Statistics will not tell you whether a century was scored on a seaming pitch against demanding bowling, or on a shirt-front wicket against a second string attack. Nor will they help you appreciate a player's style and character. To me, one of the best ways of learning about the giants of New Zealand cricket is to read what their contemporaries wrote about them. There is nothing like a few well-chosen paragraphs, by an informed and skilful writer, for creating a mental picture of the qualities that made a particular player great.

This pen-portrait of Lowry, who played test cricket for New Zealand and county cricket for Somerset, is a wonderful example of the way words can bring a famous player of the past to life.

I have an idea that the ability and performances of Tom Lowry, the New Zealander, have never received quite the notice that they deserve. For he was a most remarkable cricketer; strong, versatile, courageous, original, and a leader in a thousand. His comments on the run of the play, had they reached the spectators, would alone have justified the Entertainment Tax, and, when things went wrong, as they often did, with the Somerset batting, it was good to see him go to battle in a wicked old Homburg hat, grasping the bat-blade in his big hand, and muttering some curses about their bowling, or our own batsmen, or both. He was a man first and a cricketer second, but it was a close finish.

On to the build and the inclination of a hitter he grafted the technique and discipline of defence. You could, as it were, see the join; and there was nothing about it all that was beautiful to watch; but it could be fine to hear, when the boom of the sightscreen answered the crack of the bat. As a wicketkeeper he was tough, occasionally negligent, often brilliant, nearly always the last to arrive on the field. He would start, perhaps, rather clumsily, and miss some obvious chance, then he would wipe that out with some wonderful stumping, off an inswinger, on the blind spot just outside the leg stump. He used to bowl a little, old-fashioned off-spinners, between the fall of wickets. In later years, under his own leadership, he bowled for New Zealand at more material times.

In summer 1922, his first season in England, he somehow missed his Blue at Cambridge. As with the stumping so with this matter, the mistake was brilliantly deleted. In 1923 he reached his 1000 runs before the match against Oxford. This had never been done before. At Lord's he failed — Cambridge, on a difficult, rain-spoilt pitch, running into some great spin bowling by R.H. Bettington and G.T.S. Stevens. He played for the Gentlemen against the Players. His driving and hooking at this time were terrific, and I remember a Sussex slow bowler at Eastbourne saying to him: 'Anywhere, sir; hit 'em anywhere, but for the Lord's sake not straight back at me.' In 1924 he captained Cambridge and, playing an innings of 80, led his side to victory over Oxford by nine wickets. At the end of that season he left English County cricket, and Somerset did not find his like.

He returned three years later as captain of New Zealand, having, by the way, played against his country under A.C. Maclaren in winter 1922–23. As a cricketer he was now no less effective than before, but quieter. 'I have to save it all up,' he would say, 'for my public speeches.' In 1931 he came again, and it was in no small degree due to him and his communicated example that the tests against New Zealand have been such good games to watch and to play. Lowry would say that they came to learn. Maybe; but I think we learnt even more, absorbed as we were in averages and decimal points.

On his last visit, in 1937, he came as manager of the New Zealand team. 'They couldn't find anyone else,' he said. They couldn't, for there's only one Tom Lowry.

R.C. Robertson-Glasgow *Cricket Prints* (1943)

In a late collection of his occasional writings from the *Observer* newspaper, published under the title *More Cricket Prints,* Robertson-Glasgow turned his pen to one of New Zealand's finest batsmen, C.S. Dempster. 'His strokes' he wrote, 'have a grace seldom seen in the short and strong. He is a persuader, and smacks the ball often against the pavilion rails from a quiet-looking forward stroke. Like the few great, he kills the slow spinners with a quick foot and a confident heart.' This later profile of Dempster, written by the king of New Zealand's cricketing writers, R.T. Brittenden, is less poetically expressed but perhaps conveys more exactly the essence of the man, and his batting style.

If the Wellington City Council, one of these days, receives a small amount of conscience money, with a note explaining that the sender had been in the habit, as a small boy, of crawling through a hole in the board fence at the Basin Reserve to watch the cricket matches there, the councillors will be in a difficult position. The note would be from C.S. Dempster, and if the council, in turn, took heed of its conscience, it would have to do something about the money it owed Dempster, for he was a prime favourite at the Basin for a good many years, and did his share towards keeping the council's rates within almost manageable limits.

Dempster is associated with the Basin Reserve as firmly as Hobbs with the Oval. His illegal entries to the ground, about the time of the First World War, showed his enthusiasm for cricket. A little later, he was able to come in through the gate. He went there to practise after school, and he was there, almost throughout the summer, at six in the morning. The groundsman then was the Australian test bowler, J.V. Saunders, a kindly man who saw no reason to curb the eagerness of young Dempster and his friends.

On those dewy, unforgettable mornings, the boys would assemble at the ground for interstreet matches, their wickets chalk marks made on the heavy roller. Play ended for the morning when Saunders fitted the leather shoes on the horse and brought it out to start the rolling.

Dempster had no family background of cricket. He is of Scottish descent, and was proud, later, to play for Scotland. But there must have been some inner urge to become a good cricketer, for he was an avid watcher, and an observant one. The batsmen he liked particularly were J.S. Hiddleston, Billy Patrick and B.J. Kortlang — Kortlang, the Australian, who taught New Zealand the hook stroke. Dempster absorbed the lessons these players taught, and, with youth and confidence as firm props, he built up his technique so swiftly and so well that he was playing for Wellington at 18. Before he was 30, he was rightly regarded as the finest batsman New Zealand had ever produced.

The greater the occasion, the better Dempster seemed to respond. This may explain his comparatively modest successes in Plunket Shield cricket, compared with the remarkable results he achieved on his English tours, in county cricket and in tests. In Wellington club cricket, he scored 30 centuries in 116 innings, and had a career average of nearly 76. In one season of these Saturday afternoon games — in 1928–29 — his scores were 41, 144 not out, 123, 41, 85, 201, 139, 69, 173, 166. In all, 1182 runs at an average of 131.3.

But in Plunket Shield cricket, Dempster's average was only 35. Yet he was quite outstanding on the 1927 and 1931 tours, and in tests he had an astonishing average of 65, and there are only one or two with a better record than that.

Dempster made so many runs in the best company because he saw the ball so soon, and was able to get easily into position. Small, with a hint of the bow-legged in his walk, he looked all business at the wicket. He liked best to off-drive, but he could cut magnificently, hook savagely, glance delicately. Quick footwork, confidence in his own skill, an extraordinary ability to find the gaps, and a willingness to run the singles all contributed to making Dempster a really great player. New Zealanders have usually viewed their test teams with some distrust, but when Dempster was in, all was well with the world.

Anyone bowling short to Dempster paid heavily for his sins; all he could do was keep the ball up and hope for the best. Dempster never played at the pitch of the ball. He never had to hurry a stroke, he always seemed, like Cowdrey, to have bat and pad together, he never looked anything less than competent.

Yet when Dempster was chosen for the 1927 tour — possibly because Hiddleston was not available — his only century had been against the Melbourne Cricket Club, a second-class match, in Dempster's first appearance for New Zealand. But in England he played in 24 of the 26 first-class games, and averaged 46. In all the matches, he scored six centuries, and from that tour, he never looked back.

New Zealand had its first official tests in 1929–30, when A.H.H. Gilligan led an M.C.C. team on tour. Heavily defeated in the first match at Christchurch, New Zealand went in first at the Basin Reserve, on a pitch from which the Essex fast bowler, M.S. Nichols, made the ball rear venomously. Dempster was hit on the head. Later, his bat was knocked from his hands. His partner, Jack Mills, had his cap neatly removed by one which flew at him at fearful velocity. But they survived the assault, and by lunch had scored 113 in an hour and three-quarters. They went on down the day, Dempster scoring New Zealand's first test century, Mills following a little later, and they were not parted until they had scored 276, a New Zealand record for any wicket in a test. That summer was richly productive for Dempster, for he averaged nearly 91, and his mastery was almost absolute.

Dempster preceded the 1931 English tour with an indifferent Plunket Shield season. But once he had put on his pads at Leyton, he earned *Wisden*'s subsequent description, of being one of the best and most consistent batsmen in the world.

He started the tour with 212 against Essex — and Nichols — scored 92 and 20 not out against Leicestershire, 21 and 106 not out against Hampshire, 45 against the M.C.C., 129 not out and 5 against Glamorgan, 36 and 101 not out against Cambridge. So at the start of June he had made four centuries in six matches, and was averaging 144. This dizzy pace could not, of course, be maintained, but Dempster won the distinction of scoring New Zealand's first test century overseas — 120 at Lord's, after 53 in the first innings. And at the end of the summer, he had scored 1778 runs in the major matches, at an average of almost 60. No wonder comparisons were made with Bradman.

Dempster's finest test innings was yet to come. This was against Jardine's team, at Auckland, in 1933. Dempster batted at number four that day, but he might as well have opened, the first two wickets having fallen without a run on the board. And while the others struggled to survive against Allen, Bowes, Mitchell, Voce, Brown and Hammond, Dempster played with consummate ease. He was never in the slightest difficulty, he scored 83 of the 144 runs off the bat, and was undefeated. This was a magnificent effort. Hammond, who was better qualified to judge than most, told Dempster he would never play a better innings.

Dempster was about to leave on a business trip to England when this match was played, and he must be one of the few individuals who has had a passenger liner wait for him. The captain of the *Tainui* was a keen cricketer, and found that the ship could not leave until midnight on the day the game finished.

Although he went to England to acquire some more agencies, Dempster had so many offers to play cricket that he stayed for years. There were two or three seasons with Sir Julien Cahn's eleven; he played for Blackpool in the Ribblesdale League, and although he started late, he broke the league record aggregate.

Then he qualified for Leicestershire and led the county for several seasons. His official position with the club was 'financial secretary', an arrangement which seemed to satisfy the needs of all concerned. In his term of office, Leicestershire did little, but Dempster did much. For three full seasons, he averaged nearly 50 for the country. He became the only Leicestershire batsman to score a century against the Australians. That was in 1938. In 1937, against Gloucestershire, faultless batting brought him two centuries; twice Dempster had three consecutive centuries. When he played for services teams, during the war, he just could not stop making runs.

Dempster returned to New Zealand, and played in two more Plunket Shield series. There were centuries against Canterbury and Auckland, but he was 44, and his sight was beginning to fail him a little. In his final appearance, at Eden Park, however, he started his second innings splendidly. He intended, he said later, to make a century. But after he had been hit on an instep by John Hayes, he was sadly handicapped, and he was out for 41.

In 1957, at Cornwall Park in Auckland, Dempster made his last public appearance as a batsman, in a charity match. He opened again with Mills, and he made 11. They were good-looking runs.

Dempster was a very great batsman, and would have graced any test team in his time. So if, next season, any small boys are seen worming their way through apertures in the fence at the Basin Reserve, ground officials would be well advised to turn a blind eye. They might otherwise do the game a grave disservice.

R.T. Brittenden *New Zealand Cricketers* (1961)

The incomparable England batsman, Wally Hammond, whom John Arlott once described as 'among the half-dozen finest cricketers of all history', had a high opinion of New Zealand cricket. He admired its team-work, its fielding, its fighting spirit, and the number of quality batsmen it produced. New Zealand's problem, he felt, was that it never quite managed to make the grade in bowling. Except, of course, for the astonishing Clarrie Grimmett — whose talents, rejected by the New Zealand selectors, later flourished so emphatically for Australia.

There was something that always belonged to New Zealand in Grimmett's bowling. He was never so much at home on the Australian 'shirt fronts' as he was in England, where wickets are more like New Zealand's and the air is moist and will hold the ball much more than in Australia. There was less of the flashing genius of Australia in Clarrie than the dogged, deliberate skill of the New Zealander; and how he could work! On many occasions he bowled more than 500 balls in a test, and sometimes over 600 — a performance that will sometimes cause a bowler to lose up to a stone in weight. Occasionally, in test cricket, a bowler has topped the 700 balls, but not often — I can only recall Verity, White, and Tate. Only a lion-hearted bowler can do it.

Grimmett did not become a regular first-class cricketer till he was 32. I wonder how many other bowlers would have kept on trying, as he did, after youth was gone, still positive that they knew better than the selectors? I don't know of one! He played on and off for seven years for the Victoria Eleven, and was rejected as not up to State standard.

Having got into big cricket properly, he bowled about 73,000 balls, every one potential, and took 1402 wickets in 239 first-class games. Only one other Australian has reached the 1000 wickets, and he only passed the round figure by 12 — George Giffen. Grimmett is the only bowler of any country who has reached the 200 wickets in tests, having bagged 228, including 106 against England, 77 against South Africa, 33 against the West Indies, and 12 against his own birth-land.

They say he never bowled a long hop, and did not put up, in all his career, more than a dozen full tosses. Thinking back, I cannot recall that he ever offered me one of either. Once, when he was no-balled (in New Zealand), he said: 'Umpire, that's never happened to me before. A prophet has no honour in his own country!'

Walter Hammond *Cricket My World* (1948)

Those who failed to pick Grimmett for New Zealand must have winced at the success he enjoyed with his adopted Australia. Selectors make an easy target, especially when things go wrong, but it is only fair to acknowledge that they have sometimes been proved spectacularly right. The selection panel that chose 19-year-old Martin Donnelly for the 1937 tour of England, on the strength of just one first-class match, were more than rewarded when he came second in the batting averages. The peak of Donnelly's international career coincided with New Zealand's next tour to England, in 1949, when he formed one half of a remarkable batting double-act with the slightly younger Bert Sutcliffe.

 Both left-handers, they had different styles. Where Sutcliffe seemed to make more use of his legs and arms, Donnelly appeared to rely on his body swing and wrists, and his on-driving was executed with the face of the bat shut. Both were in their element when rapid scoring was required, and their partnerships against Hampshire and Lancashire (second match), to mention only two occasions, were models of concentration, footwork and power. They were usually called upon to play a different type of innings: Sutcliffe as opening batsman, Donnelly as number five. Of the two, Martin probably had more dour innings to play, either to hold an innings together or to mend it, a role for which he was perhaps more suited temperamentally. But to watch them hitting against the clock, Martin fiddling with his cap, patting his block; Bert, lithe and fair-haired, carrying his bat while running as though it were an umbrella, both driving and pulling with artistry — this was the pith of cricket.

Alan W. Mitchell *Cricketing Companions* (1950)

Thousands of words have been written about Donnelly and Sutcliffe and so many of them are so good that they seem designed to prove the truth of that old saying, 'quality breeds quality'. One of the most striking word pictures of the two in action is this report on the last day of New Zealand's match against Lancashire on 23 August 1949, which originally appeared in the *Manchester Guardian*.

 Those who stayed away from Lancashire's cricket match with the New Zealanders here today may well not forgive themselves for the rest of their lives. They missed not only a great victory for the New Zealanders but some of the greatest batsmanship that is likely to be seen in a generation.

Few of the spectators today could have anticipated after lunch the magnificence that was still in store for them. At a quarter to three Lancashire were 193 for 3 wickets, at five past three 218 for 4, and all that seemed left for the crowd to do was to watch some cheerful hitting by Lancashire of not always accurate bowling and to drowse on this lovely ground in the falling afternoon sunshine. Then unexpectedly at twenty past three Howard (the Lancashire captain) declared at 224 for 5 wickets. It was a fine gesture but would have seemed against most counties a reasonably safe one. It left the New Zealanders an hour and a quarter in which to score 153 runs on a dusty wicket on which neither side had scored at a much faster rate than one run a minute.

In the matter of scoring runs quickly, however, the New Zealanders are not a normal side, and when New Zealand's captain for the match, Wallace, sent in Donnelly and Sutcliffe it was certain that they would not be so today, unless one or both of them was dismissed quickly. Neither batsman committed an error for over 50 minutes. Then Donnelly jumped to drive a fast good-length ball from Tattersall, missed and was stumped easily. But the New Zealanders were 120 for 1 wicket, and when Reid dispelled any suspicion that he might fall into rashness through over-eagerness victory for the New Zealanders was assured. It came with a furious high on-drive by Sutcliffe. There were still seven minutes to spare.

It had been wonderful batting indeed that had attacked from the first ball it received. Both Sutcliffe and Donnelly drove, hooked, pulled and placed pushed shots for singles it seemed just how, when and where they might choose. Much more they did so without a hint of risk and without the giving of a chance. Only Stone at the start bowled erratically, and Greenwood, Tattersall and Hilton were about as accurate in length as they were yesterday. That the runs came as freely as they did was because wherever a ball was bowled within a length not short enough to be hooked or pulled Sutcliffe and Donnelly found its pitch. They did so by the quickest footwork that most of today's crowd will have seen. At one moment they skipped down the wicket like dancers, at another like sprinters from their starting-blocks. Sometimes a short leap would seem to propel them with the sudden fury of a missile from a catapult. But though the speed of their footwork was remarkable, the judgement which made it possible was more so. Scarcely once did either batsman miscalculate a ball's length or pace. If they did so, the withdrawal of a foot or a step backwards made like lightning would transform a drive into a brilliant hook or cut.

How confident was their judgement was seen best when Hilton was bowling. Almost at once Howard was compelled to set two long-ons and a deep mid-wicket for both of them. It reduced their drives to singles or twos immediately. Yet for nearly an hour even this could not worry them. It merely meant that if Hilton pitched outside the off-stump he was driven on the instant through the covers or past mid-off to the boundary. Hilton, indeed, was the most ruthlessly treated of all. Except when he was hooked it seemed that almost three-quarters of his balls were driven. Both batsmen jumped 5 yards, sometimes 6, to meet him and each shot, except for the high straight drive, was made along the ground and from the middle of bats which by some miracle seemed to have been deprived of edges. So sure did they seem that after the score had reached 80 all sense of a race against time vanished. Before this and after it their batting was so finely controlled that their purely defensive shots or pushes for singles did not seem outnumbered by their hits. How master they were of their task is revealed by the steadiness of their scoring. Including 11 extras the runs that came from each over were as follows: 9, 8, 5, 4, 4, 5, 6, 5, 5, 3, 2, 5, 4, 1, 14, 10, 7, 16, 4, 3, 4, 11, 2, 1, 7, 8.

Stone bowled two overs and Greenwood three. The rest were bowled by Tattersall and Hilton. Stone was as erratic as he was yesterday, and in his first over Sutcliffe and Donnelly each hooked him for singles to long-leg and Sutcliffe drove him past point for two and turned him off his toes to square-leg for four. Although Greenwood's length was much steadier he was driven more remorselessly. If he bowled on the leg-stump he was glanced and when he shortened his length he was pulled. The first 50 came in less than 25 minutes, and though Tattersall steadied the scoring appreciably and once reduced it to a single from one over it made matters only worse for Hilton: Sutcliffe twice drove the latter in his next over for fours with such casual ease that Hilton, perhaps in despair, dropped the last ball nearly at his toes. Sutcliffe hit that for four too off its second bounce and grinned as impishly as the schoolboys who were watching him. The score was now 80 after only another 15 minutes' batting. It was now Donnelly's turn and Tattersall's. Donnelly celebrated Sutcliffe's 50 out of 97 by twice driving Tattersall off his toes to mid-wicket and then with wicked venom to long-on. He and Sutcliffe next glanced him for singles with such delicacy that one felt that one's eyes had deceived one and that two balls earlier such naked violence had not been. Ten minutes later the score was 120. Donnelly at last was out, and in a quarter of an hour the game was over.

The contrast in manner of the two batsmen was as fascinating as a student of style could have asked. Sutcliffe was all easeful flow no matter how far he jumped to drive. His body leaned into and over his shots still, and he was all grace and leisure however vigorously he sometimes hit. His footwork was as light as it was rapid and made his body seem without weight, and his bat weaved this way and that more like a wand when it did not flash brilliance like a sword. Always he was smiling, elegant and unruffled, eager but not grasping, attacking but not laying waste. Even though his purpose was clear-cut and his resolution as determined as his partner's, he was always a self-conscious stylist, and he seemed to cherish each shot he made.

By contrast, Donnelly was a compact mass of savage violence. Each crack of his bat was like a hammer blow. Where Sutcliffe's shots ran into smooth lines and curves, his were close-knit, short-armed and made, it seemed, with wrists of steel. Much more than Sutcliffe he made the bowler's length what he wished it to be. He took more risks, made more creative strokes, but never did he smile. His mastery was austere and unrelenting, his mood tempered to hostility, and even his defensive shots were pouncing and dynamic. He was more calculating, too. He never wasted energy. His bat was a cudgel to be used only where and when it could do most batter. Sutcliffe would have scored consistently and charmingly off Tattersall. Only Donnelly could have shattered his length in one terrible over. So different were these two batsmen in temper, yet so alike in technical mastery, that it was impossible to subdue either of them so long as both were together. Donnelly beat the bowlers into subjection after Sutcliffe had persuaded them to error. Then Sutcliffe reaped the harvest of his partner's devastation. The like of both of them on this day may not be seen for years again.

Denys Rowbottom 'Great Batting at Aigburth', reprinted in Kenneth Gregory
In Celebration of Cricket (1978)

To be captain of New Zealand can be an unenviable task. All too often it means putting a cheerful face upon disaster, or leading gallantly from the front in pursuit of a forlorn hope. The captain of the 1949 team, Walter Hadlee, might be considered luckier than some, given the quality of many of the players under his command. But a captain makes his own luck, and that most objective of cricketing writers, John Arlott, rated Hadlee very highly. In typical Arlott fashion, this tribute ranges widely and is as much a picture of the enormously successful 1949 touring party as of the man who led it.

On a test match Monday morning in 1937 at Manchester, New Zealand went out to bat against England on a wicket made spiteful by weekend rain and in face of an English total 358. The English bowlers were Big Jim Smith, Arthur Wellard, Hammond, F.R. Brown and Tom Goddard — a powerful and varied attack supported by some brilliant fieldsmen. Half the New Zealand side was out for 119. Number six was a tall, lean, quiet young man of 22 — Walter Hadlee — who, in the words of *Wisden* 'had accomplished little up to that stage of the tour'. Not always certain in playing Wellard early on, he went coolly about his rescue innings and gradually played himself in. Then he used his height and reach in fierce driving of any ball pitched up to him. He stayed to see the score more than doubled before, in turning a ball from Wellard 'round the corner,' he slipped and kicked his wicket down. His 93 — more than a third of the runs scored from the bat in the New Zealand first innings — gave his side a fighting chance.

That coolness in trouble and courage to attack were characteristic of Hadlee's batting, and implicit in the New Zealand team he led in England in 1949. He captained that side by right, fitted as few touring captains have been for his post. He was worth his place in the side as a batsman, irrespective of whether he was captain or not — and was an experienced cricketer who had been playing Plunket Shield cricket for 17 years. Only 20 when he first played for New Zealand — against G.O. Allen's side in the M.C.C. team in 1936 — he came of age while on the tour of England in 1937. He was made captain of New Zealand against the Australians in 1945–6, and against Hammond's English team a year later. This experience, coupled with a thoughtful manner, made for real appreciation of the strategy of the game and an understanding of his men as men and players. He bridged the gap which has existed in some touring teams, between manager and players, so that his party was, in fact, a party. Here he was fortunate in having — in Jack Phillipps — a manager with a sense of humour who, like Hadlee, identified himself with the party rather than govern it from above.

If Hadlee needed to do more to establish himself among the members of his own team, he did so in the third game of the tour, against Surrey. New Zealand began their second innings on a crumbling wicket which might have been made for the Surrey bowlers. The pace of young Cox, the spin of Laker's and Eric Bedser's off-breaks and McMahon's 'Chinaman' were made doubly difficult, but most dangerous was the bowling of Alec Bedser. Bedser always has something in reserve for the wicket which really helps him, his pace seems to increase on a lively pitch, and every variation on the theme of fast-medium bowling is at his fingertips under immaculate control. On that Monday at the Oval, his leg-cutter, pitched to a blind length on the middle or middle-and-leg stumps, was darting away outside the off-stump — perfect slip-bait. Or his late inswinger would strike back at the wicket like a whiplash. The ball was lifting — often waist-high from a good length — compelling a stroke, but investing the stroke with danger. Bedser conceded less than a run an over for 30 overs. Defence alone was a full-time job on such a pitch. Yet, his left side a mass of bruises from the rising ball, Hadlee made 119 not out — no other New Zealand batsman scored more than 20. To hear the New Zealanders speak of that innings was to realise that here was that unusual cricket captain whose appointment had the unqualified approval of all his team.

The captain who really captains his side is always reflected in the character of that side. Those 1949 New Zealanders, indeed, reflected their captain's power of fighting back. In the first match of the tour, against Yorkshire, the tourists had a narrow first-innings lead when they started their second innings. Aspinall and Coxon took the new ball to dismiss the first three New Zealand batsmen with only 30 runs on the board. Reacting as Yorkshire sides do when they scent the opportunity of bustling a side out, Yorkshire fieldsmen moved up close to the wicket. It seemed that they had only to break through this fourth-wicket partnership of Wallace and Donnelly to open the door of the hutch. Wallace and Donnelly appreciated their responsibility, but they proposed to shoulder it gallantly. Bat was put hard to ball, and they were still there as the clock-hand moved into the last ten minutes before lunch — usually the slow-motion period in a county game with the batsmen taking no chances, but batting for the afternoon. John Wardle bowled his slow left-arm breakaways from the pavilion end with no fieldsman in the deep. There were only a couple of minutes to go to lunch when Wallace stepped down the wicket and let go an old-fashioned straight drive which lofted the ball high to the pavilion rails. A minute later yet another towering hit went for four, and there, unmistakably, was the stamp of the happy cricketer which has been overlaid with care in much English cricket of recent years. In subsequent matches, not only Hadlee, Wallace and

Donnelly, but also Reid, and — memorably against the M.C.C. at Lord's — Rabone and wicketkeeper Mooney, played gallant rescue innings. Hadlee's consuming enthusiasm for cricket was also reflected in his team. At Leicester, Hayes, the young fast bowler — who was not playing in the match — went down to the Leicester nets, alone, just after nine each morning. He bowled six balls at full pace at the stumps, walked down, fetched the balls back to the end of his run and bowled another flat-out over. On and on he went, experimenting with his run and working up towards the pace whose promise had won him his selection for the tour.

These New Zealanders were a team of enthusiasts: none of them could show a financial profit on the tour — in fact, some actually lost money. The easiest point for us to overlook, accustomed as we are to full-time professional cricket, is that they were Saturday-afternoon cricketers and, while this accounts for the gaiety and spontaneity of their cricket, it could also lead to problems for their captain. Cowie, Wallace, Donnelly and Hadlee had toured England before, and Martin Donnelly had played at Oxford and in English cricket for several seasons. Apart from these four, any English pro has played, in a single English season, more three-day matches than any one of the younger New Zealanders had played in his entire cricket career until the English tour. In fact, Hayes, the young fast bowler of the party, had played only three first-class matches in his life prior to the trip. This fact, with the limiting of the party to 15 players instead of the 16 or even 17 usually taken on tours, added to the menace of exhaustion and staleness.

A Saturday afternoon bowl of 25 overs is plenty for a pace-bowler, but it is also fairly unusual in New Zealand where there is a long Sunday morning in bed and a week away from cricket to put him back into trim. It is not ideal preparation for a tour of England with its 25 overs today, another 25 tomorrow, followed by a long train journey and, if the skipper loses the toss, another 25 overs the day after. No wonder such a trip seeks out the old strains and tears in Dominion bowlers' muscles.

New Zealand cricket is not rich, and it needed a financially successful tour. Moreover, because of its heavy expenses, a touring side must command larger gates than the average county match even to remain solvent. Coming after the Australians of 1948, Hadlee's men had to win their matches — and win them attractively — or seem like anticlimax, when the extra spectators would not come to see them. Meanwhile, players fresh from New Zealand had to be accustomed to the strain of week-long cricket and the vagaries of the English climate and wickets, even while they developed their strongest eleven for the tests. At the same time, too, unsuccessful players had to be nursed back into form. Veteran pace-bowler Jack Cowie was a match-winner, but he had also to be rested against the tests. These problems all tugged in different directions — yet a balance between them had to be struck. Perhaps it was fortunate that Hadlee is an accountant.

These problems have never been perfectly reconciled or solved, but, in Walter Hadlee, New Zealand had a captain as likely to solve them as all but two or three touring captains of this century. He did not solve them to the extent of winning the test rubber — I think he would have been surprised if he had — but his 1949 New Zealanders tackled them with such tenacity that England could not beat them.

John Arlott *The Echoing Green* (1952)

In a small country it is easy to suffer from delusions. We like to think our geese are swans — which is perhaps why, when some of our cricketing high-fliers get found out at international level, the reaction at home can be brutal. Considering the size of our population, the number of fine cricketers we produce is really astonishing, and it is heartening to know how highly some of them are regarded by great players from other countries.

New Zealand cricket might be cheered out of its chronic state of self-pity at news that one of the greatest of Australian batsmen, none other than Stan McCabe, considers that the greatest bowler he ever faced was the Auckland quickie, Jack Cowie. New Zealand cricket might also be cheered to learn that that very great Australian bowler, Bill O'Reilly, after almost 30 years still talks with the liveliest admiration of another Aucklander, Mervyn Wallace, who twice carted him over the fence at the Sydney Cricket Ground.

O'Reilly, a cheery card, a huge man with a pungent Irish wit, and McCabe, a pleasant man of medium height whose health recently has been indifferent, reminisced volubly about New Zealand cricket when I was introduced to them during a Sheffield Shield match at the Sydney Cricket Ground. Before McCabe joined us, O'Reilly demanded to know a good deal. What had happened to that little chap, 'Dempster' — 'he was a good 'un.' What about Giff Vivian — and being himself a left-hander, Bill seemed more than satisfied to learn that Vivian's left-handed golfing of the moment is much more often victorious than inglorious…

'I well remember our tour of New Zealand in 1946, at the end of the war,' O'Reilly said. 'Our Board of Control would not recognise us as a full Australian team. They called us the "ABC" team. We talked of ourselves as the "Australian Battle Contingent". During the tour, some Kiwi told us we must be representing the Auckland Bottle Company. We loved that. Any time any of us get together, we always talk about the Auckland Bottle Company team.'

O'Reilly's mind darted off. 'Then there was that big bloke in the 1937 Kiwi team,' he said. 'Cowie. Jack Cowie. You ought to ask Stan McCabe about him. Rolled him twice. In only three balls.' He chuckled mirthfully. His 15 st 10 lb frame shook with glee at the memory of the Master Batsman, McCabe, suffering from a little-known New Zealander. He seemed not quite so pleased when McCabe joined us at the tail of this memory. Having heard 'Tiger' so often taking the mickey out of others, McCabe swept to the attack.

'That New Zealand fellow, Wallace, "Tiger",' he asked innocently, 'you'd remember him? Twice over the fence, wasn't it?'

'I certainly do,' said O'Reilly. 'I always did have the power of speech. I never liked going over the fence, even once. Twice from the same man. I said quite a bit. That kid could really hit.'

'All the same,' said McCabe, 'Wallace was very silly. I was fielding square. Wallace kept hoisting them over me. Every time he did this, I dropped back a yard or so. "Tiger", you tossed one at him and there it was — down my throat. If only Wallace hadn't been so eager…' He sounded regretful in the manner of one artist not quite forgiving another, even though he understood the momentary flaw.

'Yeah,' said O'Reilly. 'Wallace holed out. But what about you and that big bloke, Cowie? Remember that?'

'Do I what?' said McCabe. He turned to me. Even after 29 years, it was evident his memory was razor-sharp — could Cowie command a finer tribute?

'First innings, I went first ball,' said McCabe. 'Cowie bowled me an inswinger. It was tremendous. I didn't even see it. When it had passed through, I didn't need to be told what had happened. A magnificent ball. Second dig, I was pretty hot. I was going to get this cove. His first ball was another tremendous inswinger. I groped for it and missed it clean. It went across my body, down the leg side.

'Next one, Cowie pitched dead on the middle stump. With that action, it couldn't be anything else but another inswinger. I shaped to play the ball to leg. Nothing to it. I had everything covered.

'Do you know, I was actually playing the stroke around the corner when the ball whipped from the pitch and clipped my off-bail. The perfect outswinger — me going one way, the ball the other.'

O'Reilly chuckled. 'He rolled you. Twice in three balls. He rolled you.'

'He certainly did,' said McCabe. 'I hate him. No — that's not right. I don't hate him now. But I did — for a long, long time. And I still say he was the greatest bowler I ever faced.'

T.P. McLean 'Aussie Greats Remember Kiwi Cricket Stars', *New Zealand Herald* 19 November 1966, reprinted in *The Best of McLean* (1984)

The genuine all rounder is surely the darling of the gods: never out of the game, and always able to compensate for an ignominious duck by taking a few cheap wickets. Armchair cricketers of the 1950s and '60s thrilled to the exploits of J.R. Reid and hundreds of school-age players, up and down the country, tried to imitate his trade-mark pull shot, only to lose their wickets when they failed to connect with the ball. Reid smashed national cricketing records with the same aggressive fluency that he displayed when batting, bowling and fielding. He could even keep wicket when necessary. When times were lean, it often seemed as if he was carrying the whole burden of New Zealand's cricketing fortunes on his shoulders, but he had his reward in better times, when he led his country to its first three test match victories — and broke the psychological barrier to cricketing success in the process.

John Reid graduated to captaincy the hard way, if ever a skipper did. As a schoolboy, to quote an admirer, he 'played himself silly', turning out for representative school sides at both cricket and rugby football. Twice rheumatic fever painfully intervened and, as though that were not enough, he managed to put his shoulder out, but the latter disabling accident merely made him turn to wicketkeeping as an innocuous pastime until he was fit to bowl again. It now seems a slightly grim joke that he had to give up rugger, because rheumatic fever as a parting gift had left him with a weak heart, but at the age of 18 he was playing cricket for the Wellington club. Two years later he came to England as a very junior member of W.A. Hadlee's side.

Hadlee's tour of 1949 has left more than one clear memory behind: in the first place, the New Zealanders held England to a draw in all four tests played, and though their bowling never became deadly in that batsman's golden summer, their fielding was a joy to watch. In this eager and prehensile fielding side Reid was singled out by *Wisden* as the best of a superb lot. He was also able to use his other gift with the gloves, when the regular wicketkeeper received an injury. His bowling was sparingly used, though, when his captain did put him on, he bowled at lightning speed. As a junior member of the team he did not make his test debut until the third. This was played at Old Trafford, and from the first moment he showed that he possessed the big match temperament by instantly stopping a collapse, scoring a steady half century, and holding one end firm, thus enabling the brilliant Donnelly to play his own free game at the other. Promoted to the number three position at the Oval, he failed in the first innings but gave a finely aggressive display in the second, missing his hundred by only seven runs.

Back home at the end of the tour, he helped his own team, Wellington, to win the Plunket Shield, showing his skill with both ball and bat by such contributions as 5 for 20 against Canterbury and 82 and 112 against Auckland. And so it went on, with a test 50 against F.R. Brown's team when they came over on their way home from Australia, and he followed this with still further outstanding all-round play in Plunket Shield matches. In 1951–2, still playing for Wellington, he not only made the highest score of his career, which was 283, against Otago, but, in case they had not been previously impressed, took five wickets for 35. Oddly enough, in spite of these feats and the hitting of another bright hundred against Auckland, his team finished at the bottom of the Shield table.

Reid spent the next three English summers in Lancashire, where no doubt he found the climate different from that of his sunny native land, but this did not deter him from taking a hundred wickets each season and scoring 1300 runs in the third. He was no more than a few odd runs short of the double on the other two occasions. He was naturally picked to tour South Africa in 1953–4 under G.O. Rabone, and to visit Pakistan and India two years later. On this first tour his was easily the first name in all the records, taking the palm as an all-rounder by scoring 1012 runs and capturing 51 wickets, a record that had never been beaten in the South African season. He did nothing in the first two tests, but scored a glorious 135 in the third, an innings which many thought the finest, and certainly most aggressive, played by anyone during the whole series.

The test matches of 1955 were for New Zealand a marathon. There was an element of non-stop variety in the whole thing; they played 12 in such succession: three in Pakistan, five in India and four, on their return home, against the West Indies. During the whole of this endurance test, for which any honest trade unionists might have claimed danger money, Reid was New Zealand's sheet-anchor; the difference was that in batting and bowling he showed qualities not usually associated with the anchor man: the power to hit aggressively and to bowl very fast. In the whole of the tour he once more headed the batting with three centuries. In the bowling, with a bag of 39 wickets, which was far higher than anyone else's, he came second to Harford, who in any event had taken only four. It was in the twelfth of these successive battles that New Zealand gained their first international victory in 26 years of test cricket. (It had been in the tenth out of this long-distance dozen that he had taken over the captaincy and in this game he had fought a truculent rearguard action, making top score in each innings.) The last game of the series saw New Zealand triumph at last and their new captain with them, for, though there had been some skilful bowling from both sides, it was Reid's first innings (84), freely hit out of a partnership of 112 for the sixth wicket, that virtually retrieved the situation. So, in a true sense, Reid could be regarded as New Zealand's most successful captain.

He led the New Zealand side in England in 1958 and needed all his optimism almost literally to keep his team's head above water, a task not eased by the woeful wetness of the season. Much of New Zealand's batting was irritably slow, but his was not. Such was his devotion to duty, always eager but never grim, that he played in 28 of the side's 31 first-class matches. (This type of devotion recalls another New Zealand hero, the Maori, George Nepia, who as fullback in the All Blacks rugby team of 1924–5 played in every match of the tour.) Unfortunately the example Reid set was not regularly followed by his team and they gained, perhaps unfairly for some, the reputation of being defensive in outlook to excess. This defensive complex no doubt has something to do with their loss of four tests and of their being saved by rain and Reid — by his aggressive 51 not out at the Oval — in the fifth.

He accomplished scarcely anything against May's team that came on from Australia in 1958–9, but he once more showed himself a tower of strength in combating the Australians, led by Ian Craig, who visited New Zealand in

1960–1. In the four representative matches played — they were not regarded as official tests — he scored 292, at an average of 36. Apart from one sterling century by Sutcliffe and a couple of sturdy fifties by Sparling, there were hardly any individual scores, except Reid's, on the New Zealand side which were worth remembering. Reid also did little, except for one masterly 83, against D.W. Silk's 'A' team, but fate seemed to have been grooming him for New Zealand's tour of South Africa.

The tests played on this tour were perforce regarded as unofficial, because of South Africa's withdrawal from the Commonwealth, but, as the Imperial Conference of 1962 agreed, there appeared to be no reason why matches played by South Africa should not be called tests, even though the Imperial Conference did not recognise them as official.

Of this series John Reid, if he could momentarily conquer his natural modesty, could undoubtedly admit that it was his finest hour. It was, in fact, New Zealand's finest rubber, too; hitherto, they had won only one test match; in South Africa they went on to win two more and, though they also lost two, drawing the fifth ensured that they eventually succeeded in drawing the series. If Reid had been the prop and stay of his side in the years before, in this tour he was unchallenged master. In batting he not only headed the tables in tests and all first-class matches, but averaged twice as many runs as the next man. His tour aggregate was little under 2000 runs; while Dowling's, the next highest, was 715. This total, in fact, was the highest ever amassed by a tourist in South Africa, even beating Compton's in 1948–9, and May's in 1956–7. Not only did Reid score seven hundreds; he enhanced his reputation as a close fielder with 22 catches. If he took only 11 wickets in the five tests he undoubtedly took them at a lower cost than anybody else, and it was in the vital fifth test at Port Elizabeth, which New Zealand excitingly won by 40 runs to square the rubber, that his bowling played the vital part. New Zealand led by 85 on the first innings, but the second innings crumbled and Reid was the one who characteristically came in at a moment of crisis, helped the admirable Dowling in putting on 125 for the fourth wicket and thus eventually hauled New Zealand's score back to respectability. The real crunch came in the fourth innings of the match and here South Africa fought every inch of the way. With the 100 on the board for one wicket they were on the firm road to victory; at 142 for 6 they had been brought to the edge of defeat. It was the obstinate ninth-wicket partnership between Peter Pollock and Adcock which threatened to snatch victory from the jaws of defeat. During this painfully palpitating innings Reid bowled over after over with deadly accuracy and a cunning variation not usually associated with bowling of his speed. His figures of 45 overs, 27 maidens, 44 runs, 4 wickets tell more clearly than words the effect he had on this final innings. At last, when the new ball became due, he brought on the two bowlers who were faster than himself and they took the last wickets between them. Even then Reid's career was not ended. When Dexter's team, unsuccessful in Australia, came on to play New Zealand, he scored 80 for once out in the first test, failed in the second, and in the third boldly defied the invaders, first with a well-hit 74, and then, although Trueman was on the rampage, with a 100 of which any batsman alive might have been proud, out of a full total of 159.

It is impossible to praise John Reid too highly. More than any other captain he has struggled against adversity, standing like a giant among ordinary mortals above his colleagues without losing the friendly power to bring them along to the best of their powers and sometimes further. A splendid back-foot batsman, a fast-medium bowler of far more than ordinary skill and versatility, and one of the safest close fieldsmen in the world, he started so early that he has had almost as long a career as anyone now playing test cricket. At 36 he still has a lot of cricket before him, and may still surprise us all.

A.A. Thomson *Cricket: The Great Captains* (1965)

When Walter Hammond, in 1948, lamented New Zealand's lack of top quality bowling, he surely did not dream that the problem would be a continuing one. Some outstanding talents have played for this country since then — along with a lot of honest triers and single-season tearaway wonders — but very few New Zealand-born bowlers have emerged to rank with Grimmett in the eyes of the world.

Perhaps the most sophisticated fast bowler of them all…was not a West Indian, an Australian, a Pakistani or an Englishman, but a New Zealander. In his youth, Richard Hadlee was as wild as any other would-be quick, hurling down the ball as fast as he could and grossly overdoing the bouncer. He was stereotypical of his breed: obsessed by his own skill, that of being able to propel a cricket ball quickly, he forsook all others. He was aggressive, bullying, selfish, uncontrolled and uncontrollable. He was fiercely envious of his elder brother Dayle, who preceded him into the

Canterbury and New Zealand teams, so much so that he once announced to the rest of the family that he intended to 'bring [Dayle's] head home on a silver platter'.

But then one day, around 1980, Hadlee suddenly — and inexplicably to most people's eyes — changed. He decided he was wasting his time trying to blast out opponents. He was lean and unmuscled, gained most of his speed from a side-on delivery and a long, whippy bowling arm, and had the strength to bowl at high speed only in short bursts. He decided that, in that case, he needed to pick off his victims rather than blow them away. So he revised his methods. He cut down his run-up, employed the bouncer only as a weapon of surprise, and replaced the verbals with a stare. He bowled wicket-to-wicket, developed the ability to move the ball either way and concentrated on rhythm and swing. He spent hours studying videos of the world's best batsmen, searching for chinks in their armour, and analysing the methods of Lillee, the bowler he most admired. And it worked. If the ball could swing, he would make it; if there was anything in the pitch, he would find it; a combination of the two, and he would be absolutely deadly.

At this time, when the whole cricketing world was obsessed with knocking each other's heads off, this was a remarkable thing for anyone to do. Many New Zealanders were appalled at Hadlee's volte-face. They had come to rely on him running in off 20 yards to kick ass on behalf of a test team that spent a lot of time having its own ass kicked. Don Cameron, one of their leading cricket reporters, bemoaned 'New Zealand's heaviest artillery operating off a pop-gun run-up', a jibe that stung even Hadlee. Hadlee has often been described as a solitary man — as New Zealand's one bowler of match-winning potential he inevitably had to be — but in this respect Hadlee chose the solitary course. He was the tearaway fast bowler who turned his back on the greatest bun fight in cricket history to ply his trade as seam-up-and-swing-it merchant. Hadlee could not have surprised people more if he had announced he was going off to join the local ballet company.

For the last ten years of his career, Hadlee ploughed his lonely furrow. He was known as a ruthless operator. Derek Randall said he could be 'one of the nastiest pieces of work I have come across'; Greg Matthews described him as 'one of the most aggressive bowlers I've ever faced. He uses eye contact — he has a presence'. Although he did once give Peter Roebuck a working over after Roebuck had described him in a newspaper article as 'austere and morose', and he had his inevitable run-ins with Botham, he largely eschewed the rough stuff in favour of more constructive behaviour. He occasionally played difficult, sometimes with his own team-mates, perhaps because, as David Gower once observed, 'he tired of being considered a quiet man'.

But at the end of it all, Hadlee got what he wanted. He did not want to hit a batsman between the eyes as he stretched defensively forward; he did not want to hit him in the teeth after deceiving him with a quick bouncer; he had no desire to break fingers, thumbs or ribs. He simply wanted to be top of the pile. Not the fastest, not the scariest, just the best.

And in the end, he was.

Simon Wilde *Letting Rip* (1994)

Like Hadlee, New Zealand's two best batsmen of recent times, Glenn Turner and Martin Crowe, have chosen their own paths. In the 1970s, when New Zealand enjoyed its longest run of international cricketing success, Turner's batting skill and record-breaking feats stood out. For cool and steady maximising of potential he can have had few equals. Perhaps Turner was better appreciated in England, where he played so much of his cricket, than he was at home. In 1982 he hammered a 100 before lunch and another before tea, on his way to scoring a not-out triple century in a single day. It was the hundredth first-class century of his career and *The Times* celebrated the achievement with a reflective piece on his qualities as a player.

Of the 19 cricketers to have scored 100 first class hundreds none can have been more of a perfectionist than Glenn Turner, or have reached the landmark in a more spectacular way than when he scored 311 not out in one day against Warwickshire last Saturday.

He has no time for the slovenly, whether in his own game or anyone else's. As a young man he dedicated himself to developing a technique based on the teachings of the textbook, realizing that was the surest way of achieving consistency. A career average of 50, as near as makes no matter, shows how successful he has been.

To be such a very good player and yet find it necessary to score 239 not out against a weak Oxford University attack, as he did in his first innings this season, tells, as well as anything could, of Turner's single-mindedness. Some of Worcestershire's later batsmen were hoping for an early-season knock. Yet by doing things his way Turner wins more matches for them in a season than even Vivian Richards does for Somerset. That this is so is an indication of how over the years he has widened the scope of his game.

In his time he has twice carried his bat through a test innings, with infinite patience and in vastly different conditions, and yet so dominated an attack in a county championship match (Worcestershire v. Glamorgan at Swansea in 1977) as to score 141 not out out of a total of 169, a record in percentage terms. In most recent seasons he has made a habit of scoring at least 100 before lunch.

Only Walter Hammond has ever scored a hundred in each innings of a match more often than Turner. Hammond did it seven times to Turner's six. Turner's ten hundreds in a season (1970) for Worcestershire constitute a record for the county.

In 1973 he became the seventh and last batsman and the only one since the last war to score 1000 runs before the end of May. In the West Indies in 1971–2, playing for New Zealand, he scored 672 runs in the test series at an average of 96. In successive innings in Georgetown, against Guyana and then in the fourth test match, he scored 259, and batted altogether for nearly 22 hours. So one could go on.

Turner was born in Dunedin, in the South Island of New Zealand, in 1947. He was 35 on May 26, and now that he has put his 100th hundred in the bag he will probably retire at the end of the season. Once Billy Ibadulla, then coaching in New Zealand, had persuaded him to try his luck in England soon after leaving school, Turner's course was set. Besides being fastidiously correct, for a long time he was tediously slow. Yet today, of all the batsmen playing first class cricket, he makes as good a model as any for youngsters to study.

If he has not been a great success as a captain it may be because of the permissiveness of the age: he sets higher standards both on and off the field than many today find acceptable. He made no secret of his distaste for the way some of the Australians played the game in New Zealand when they were there in 1974, or for the antics of the West Indians, also in New Zealand, in 1980.

It was unlike him when, to show the West Indians what he had thought of them then, he refused to bat properly while playing for Worcestershire against them soon afterwards. It would have been in character had he kept them in the field for a couple of days with an immaculate display of manners and batting method.

In New Zealand there are those who feel, not altogether surprisingly, that he should have made himself available to play for them more often. His last test match was in 1976 when he was only 29. He has preferred in recent years to spend his time out there in the commentary box rather than at the wicket, watching far less good players trying to cope. Because of this he has never proved himself at the highest level against the fiercest pace. Some say he never could, though I disagree with that.

His record entitles him to be ranked as the foremost right-handed batsman New Zealand has produced (Martin Donnelly and Bert Sutcliffe, both great players, stood the other way round) and with such character, determination and technique he could, I am sure, have made a hundred against Holding at one end and Roberts at the other.

John Woodcock 'Turner: Man of Principle and a Perfectionist', *The Times* 2 June 1982, reprinted in *Double Century: 200 Years of Cricket in* The Times (1985)

That appreciation was written before the end of Turner's playing career. By contrast, this tribute to the greatest New Zealand batsmen of the last decade, Martin Crowe, appeared a few days after he announced his retirement.

Grown men cry more often than they like to let on. To cover such an unmanly trait, they try to conceal it with a cough or a sneeze or complain about something in an eye.

There was a fair bit of coughing and sneezing and eye-complaining when Martin Crowe said he would no longer be striding out into the middle with that brisk walk of his, anxious to get on with the business of breaking bowlers' spirits.

He had a hurried throat-clearing a few times when he talked first to Bryan Waddle on *Sports Roundup* about why he was stopping.

There was more as the day wore on, and not just from him.

Some callers to talkback radio even had to use Neil Diamond's phrase, 'a cry in the voice' when they felt the need to make public their misery and these were the types of callers who would normally bark out such manly phrases as 'up the guts' or 'stick it to 'em'.

To listen to some of the comments on Tuesday and yesterday, it was as if Crowe had died. Instead, it was a bit of cricket that had died.

Others will rattle off the statistics of tests and one-dayers played and centuries scored, and others will remember the grace and beauty of Crowe in the full range of his mastery almost disdainfully placing the ball where he wanted it.

I remember some of his innings, some of his triumphs and some of his dismissals, but mostly I remember him walking out to bat amid an expectant air I'm sure was shared, reluctantly, by the team in the field. It's a long way between a first ball and a test hundred, but sometimes there was almost an inevitability about Crowe's time at the crease, a pre-ordained order of proceedings that comes to few batsmen.

It's easy to forget that Crowe was more than a batsman. Until he had back problems, the first in a long string of ills and injuries, he was a test-quality medium pace bowler and, in his fitness prime, was athletic excellence in the field.

Crowe's career has also been one of regrets. There's a regret that for so long his real and imagined personal life seemed to be talked about more than his cricket, regret that injury so blighted his career, and most of all regret that for all his achievements, he never fulfilled the extremely high expectations we placed on him, and he on himself. Seventeen test centuries was great; it could have been much more.

There's regret that he's bowed to the inevitable and some say he could have struggled on. Maybe he could have.

For some reason, a comment made by *The Times* about a notable British Labour Party figure of the '60s and '70s, George Brown, has stuck in my mind. Brown was known to have a beer on a hot day and one day he'd had a few too many, day turned into night and he was found tired and emotional in a gutter outside the House of Commons. You can imagine what a meal the British tabloids made of this, but *The Times* took a different line. 'George Brown drunk,' it thundered, 'would have made a better prime minister than Harold Wilson sober.'

Martin Crowe on one leg would still be better than most batsmen on two.

Ron Palenski 'A bit of cricket died the day Crowe called it quits',
Dominion 18 January 1996.

As I finished compiling this anthology in July 1996, the New Zealand women's cricket team ended a truimphant tour of England. Their success was hardly a surprise, because our women cricketers have been performing wonders for decades. After all, they first scored a test match victory over Australia in 1972, a year before the men accomplished that feat and in the centenary season of 1995 — to quote a male writer in the *Sunday Star/Times* — they 'stoically defended New Zealand's reputation as a cricketing nation, while the men were being rolled over by almost anyone who could muster 11 men on any given day'. The 1996 tour of England added further lustre to the name of one New Zealander who is already considered among the greatest ever to have played the game.

When the voters for the annual Halberg Awards do their stuff this year, women's cricketer Debbie Hockley should be near the top of their lists. Hockley could be easily overlooked — she plays a minor sport and, compared to male cricketers, the All Blacks, netballers and leading Olympians, has a tiny media profile — but she is arguably the best bat in world women's cricket. She has scored the most runs of any woman in one day cricket (2417), is third on the all-time test list and has the highest combined test/one-day runs total.

New Zealand has had some fine women cricketers: Phyl Blackler, the Canterbury all-rounder, played for New Zealand for 25 years; Trish McKelvey captained New Zealand from 1966 to 1982 and scored two test centuries; there was the multi-talented Judi Doull and Jill Saulbrey, the Ewen Chatfield of the women's arena…but, for me, none of them matches Hockley… Even if she didn't play again, her place in women's cricket history would be secure, especially after her recent efforts for Sarah Illingworth's team in England. After opening this current tour with 41 and 56 not out (off 38 balls), Hockley utterly dominated the one-day series. Three times she top-scored, completing her sequence with a brilliant century, to finish the three matches with 246 runs. Each time, she ushered New Zealand to victory and was named player of the match. In England, they are jokingly referring to her as the female Bradman.

For someone who was only 15 when first selected for New Zealand — she learnt she had passed School Certificate while touring Australia in 1979 — Hockley has been through testing times. At 21, she was far too young when she was entrusted with the captaincy in 1984 and, for several years, she alternated with Lesley Murdoch in the position. The see-sawing continued in 1992, when Auckland veteran Karen Plummer was controversially promoted to the captaincy. Now Illingworth leads the team, but Hockley says that is no longer an issue. 'I'm enjoying not being captain,' she says, 'especially on a trip like this one. I wouldn't fancy all the responsibility of selecting the team, attending the meetings, the speeches and so on. It's nice to enjoy my cricket.'…

Pressed for career highlights, Hockley nominates 1987, when New Zealand won the Shell Rosebowl, and 1994, when they beat Australia in dramatic circumstances. 'We won that series 2–1. It came down to the last ball. They needed two runs and Julie Harris bowled Chris Matthews. That was a real high.'

But what about personal records, such as becoming the first New Zealander to reach 1000 runs in tests, and gaining the world one-day record, and so on?… 'Well no, not really. I mean, it was a huge buzz on this tour beating England 3–0. We'd never beaten them and had never won any series 3–0. That's where the satisfaction lay. We came over here in 1993 and lost the World Cup final at Lord's, so to beat England was a nice bit of revenge. I savoured playing at Lord's this time. In 1993 it was all a rush, but this time we practised there three times and really felt we belonged. Women were allowed into the pavilion, which was significant. There was a good crowd; it was a special day.'

Records in women's cricket can be misleading. The English legend, Rachel Heyhoe-Flint, holds the world test record with 1594 runs. Jeanette Brittin is second, about 100 runs behind and Hockley is third. But before the current series, Hockley had played just 16 tests, far fewer than the two Englishwomen, and scored 1007 runs. She is averaging nearly 50 per test innings.

Hockley has been outstanding in domestic cricket. At a national tournament in 1989 she scored 423 runs, 115 more than the next best, and in 1991 her 350 runs included two unbeaten centuries and came at an average of 116 an innings. The next year she bettered even this Sutcliffe-like performance with 369 runs at 123. And Hockley has been just as good at international level. She has been able to bat for long periods to save a match, as when scoring an unbeaten 126 against Australia at Cornwall Park in 1990 to help save the follow-on, and she can be brutally punishing — a powerful, front-foot player, not afraid to loft the ball.

So far, she is not talking retirement. 'Apparently people have been mentioning my retiring. That never came from me. I take each year as it comes. I doubt I'll come back to England to play, because we might not tour here for another five years, but I'm loving my cricket and hope to be around for a while yet.'

Joseph Romanos 'Crème de la cricket' *New Zealand Listener* 13 July 1996

Being an armchair selector seems to be a favourite cricketing pastime. Every year, when the time comes to choose the New Zealand team, the talkback telephone lines of *Sports' Roundup* run hot with callers eager to give advice, or read out their own preferred eleven. Choosing a composite team from all those who have ever worn the silver fern is an equally fascinating game. The first five or six players are easy to pick, but just who should fill the remaining places can be a matter of endless argument. Sometimes it is best to let an impartial observer resolve the debate…

The New Zealand cricketers have always been welcome visitors to Britain. Once the cynics might have attributed that to the fact that they invariably lost to England. That, though, can no longer be adduced since they beat England at Wellington in 1978. Indeed, they gained the right to take on the world when they beat Australia at Christchurch in 1974; they have now beaten all their test opponents and they emphasized their standing — at least for those who accept the criterion of the limited-overs game — in the recent World Series Cup competition in Australia. Then they had the ill-luck to go into the finals without Richard Hadlee, one of the finest fast-bowler allrounders in the game, who was injured.

There the weakness in New Zealand's representative cricket has generally lain; not in the quality of their best players but in their numbers. Producing a side capable of taking on the other cricketing nations is a considerable achievement for not merely the smallest test-playing country but one which, with a population of 3,160,000, is smaller than even a single city of each of the others, except the West Indies and Sri Lanka.

The cricket relationship between Britain and New Zealand, diagonally distant across the world, has been surprisingly good, especially by comparison with the attitude of Australia. England have consistently sent out touring teams, despite the distance and economic difficulties. After the tiring tour of Australia the continuation to New Zealand for, often, three tests and a few other matches must often have seemed Pelion piled upon Ossa to weary English cricketers. Those visits, though, have invariably been friendly and enjoyable — at least, ever since 1877, when poor Ted Pooley of Surrey was arrested and, when he should have been keeping wicket in the first test ever played between England and Australia, was languishing in a Christchurch gaol.

Australia, on the other hand, has appeared a poor — even contemptuous — neighbour. In 1929–30 England sent the team under Harold Gilligan which, on 10 January 1930, at Lancaster Park, Christchurch, ushered New Zealand into test cricket with the first of a four-match series. England and New Zealand had already played twelve tests in four series before Australia sent Bill Brown's party on a four-week, one-test tour in 1945–46. The two countries did not meet in Australia, however, until 1973–74: and in a return rubber — played, all but incomprehensibly, after so many blank years, in the same season — New Zealand achieved their first win in only the sixth match between the two. It was a hard-fought game; decided by Turner, who scored a century in each innings; Richard Hadlee (7 for 130), his brother Dayle (5 for 117), Richard Collinge (5 for 107) and some fine catching. Unhappily the New Zealanders had to endure a degree of 'sledging' — the current term for abuse and obscenity directed at opponents — which nearly marred the national celebrations of their triumph, and still rankles with some of them. Glenn Turner is an extremely independent-thinking man; and certainly the only test cricketer to be married twice on the same day. By immense thought, and initial concentration on defence, he lifted himself from an ordinary to a world-class batsman, and his career certainly ought not yet to be ended.

A few Australian teams had been there before: though never for a test match. In 1905, for instance, Darling's side sharpened up for their English tour with six matches (two against odds) there. They won four of them by an innings and drew the other two. *Wisden* — in a two-page 'summary of the matches, together with the batting and bowling averages' — contrived never to mention the name of a single New Zealand player.

Tradition recalls, though, that at Auckland the doughty Bill Stemson, opening the bowling for the local eleven, knocked out Victor Trumper's leg stump with his first ball — at the very moment that the umpire called 'no-ball'. Stemson, like the Hon. Frederick Beauclerk bowling at Tom Walker of Hambledon a century and a half before — 'off went his hat…dash upon the ground'. Trumper continued to make 92: better than his average for the tour, which was 89.66.

New Zealand have progressed far since the day in 1914 when Victor Trumper scored 293 in 180 minutes against Canterbury; and particularly since the Second World War. Several of their inter-war players came into the English county game. Stewart Dempster, who captained Leicestershire from 1936 to 1938, was an extremely accomplished opening batsman; immaculately straight in defence, a powerful driver and a product of his time in the strength of his onside play. In a New Zealand team of all periods, he would go in first with Glenn Turner. Bill Merritt played several seasons of league cricket for

Dudley and, with Ken James the wicketkeeper, for Northamptonshire. Merritt spun the leg-break and googly very sharply, if not particularly accurately; on his day, though, he was almost unplayable. On the 1931 tour, for instance, he amazed some knowledgeable critics when he took the new ball in the second innings of an extremely strong M.C.C. batting side and, making it loop and turn, took 7 for 28 to give New Zealand an innings win.

Tom Lowry, the Cambridge Blue and capable wicketkeeper-batsman who captained the 1931 team to England, also turned out for Somerset. R.C. Robertson Glasgow used to declare that he qualified on the grounds that he was born in Wellington; and no one ever asked him whether he meant Wellington, Somerset or Wellington, New Zealand.

The touring team of 1949 was exceptionally well-equipped in batting. That fact decided the outcome of the rubber. When the fixture list was first drafted they were offered three four-day tests. That astute accountant, Walter Hadlee, pointed out that such a programme would involve six blank — and therefore uneconomic — days at the best part of the summer; and he opted for four of three days each. When that was agreed, he remarked drily, 'There is not much doubt that our batting is good enough to draw all four of them.' And it was so.

That side included the finest left-hand batsman of the post-war era in Martin Donnelly. Short, neat, quick on his feet, able to dominate the best bowling by controlled aggression and a wide range of strokes, he prompted C.B. Fry to the comment that no left-hander of his time was better. Wally Hammond said laconically that he was 'one of the few really great ones'. That was high praise indeed; but justified. He had toured England with their 1937 team when he was only 19 and played some courageous defensive innings in a losing team. After the war he took a postgraduate course at Oxford and joined the touring party of 1949. His 206 in the Lord's test, still the highest score for New Zealand against England, was a masterly perfor-mance, with 26 fours and absolutely flawless until he passed 200 and started to take risks. He captained the university; but when, after a few games for Warwickshire and one for Middlesex, he took up a business appointment in Australia, he was much missed at many levels. He was, too, a brilliant rugby stand-off, capped for England while he was up at Oxford. In addition he was a man of much personal charm; an easy, relaxed manner, and a sense of humour which ranged from the dry to the zany.

If Donnelly was the finest left-hander of the era, his fellow New Zealander, Bert Sutcliffe, must challenge Neil Harvey for the next place. Splendidly athletic, an upstanding fluent strokeplayer, he had been in first-class cricket less than three years when he came with Walter Hadlee's team to England. Yet only Bradman among visiting batsmen had ever bettered his aggregate of 2627 runs (at 59.70) on that tour. He scored over 50 in five of his seven test innings; Donnelly in five out of six. Indeed, that 1949 side made even more runs than Bradman's powerful Australians of 1948. Neither were Donnelly and Sutcliffe alone; Mervyn Wallace all but achieved the feat of a thousand in May. When they beat Surrey at the Oval, Walter Hadlee played an innings of consummate skill: 119 not out in a total of 249 against Alec Bedser bowling his leg-cutters explosively on a dusty wicket.

That was the first tour of John Reid, the strong man; only 20 when he reached England, he scored 50 in his first test innings and went on to a career total of 3428 runs in tests. At one juncture he held the New Zealand test records of scoring most runs, most centuries, taking most wickets, holding most catches, playing in most matches, and captaining most often. He set the record by appearing in 58 and captaining in 34 consecutive tests. A useful fast-medium bowler, he frequently kept wicket; and was an outstanding fieldsman anywhere. A mighty driver and hooker, his 15 sixes in an innings for Wellington against Northern Districts (1962–63) has never been equalled. He batted with great courage and determination, especially during the 1950s in a series of weak teams which he often seemed to carry on his shoulders.

A representative New Zealand side which began its batting with Turner, Dempster, Sutcliffe, Donnelly would trouble any bowling side whether they followed them with the doggedly and valuably resistant Bev Congdon or Geoff Howarth (another to score a century in each innings of a test). Then would come the all-rounders, John Reid, the other strong man, the tall, combative Bruce Taylor, and, of course, the highly talented Richard Hadlee. With Botham, Kapil Dev and Imran Khan, Hadlee completes a remarkable current vintage of all-rounders. Spin bowling had generally been New Zealand's weakness; but a good selector will settle for their best — Hedley Howarth, a class slow left-arm bowler who played too little cricket, and Bill Merritt (just ahead of Roger Blunt, who was the better bat). The irrepressible and lightning-fast Frank — 'Starlight' — Mooney or the tragic Ken Wadsworth would keep wicket — if a specialist was chosen.

It is tempting, though, in that 'all-periods' team, to play John Reid as wicketkeeper and bring in an extra batsman or a pace bowler in Jack Cowie or Dick Motz, both immense triers at right-arm fast-medium; or the slightly quicker Richard Collinge to impart left-arm variety. On the other hand, remembering how well Reid bowled when the side was in trouble, his versatility in bowling, fast-medium outswing or, on a favourable wicket, off-cutters, and his fine close catching, the specialist goes in.

So the team, in batting order, would be Stewart Dempster, Glenn Turner, Bert Sutcliffe, Martin Donnelly, Geoffrey Howarth or Bev Congdon, John Reid, Bruce Taylor, Richard Hadlee, Frank Mooney, Hedley Howarth, Bill Merritt. They would be talented, entertaining and generous opponents; and extremely good company.

John Arlott, 'New Zealand Power', **Wisden Cricket Monthly** April 1983, reprinted in

Arlott on Cricket edited by David Rayvern Allen (1984)

Arlott chose his ideal New Zealand team in 1983, from the players he had seen during a lifetime's close involvement with the game. If he had ever experienced Sid Smith in action, he would surely have found him a place in the eleven.

Sid Smith was the classic schoolboy cricketing hero. He was in his prime around 1911, when he was 12 years old. He was also a completely fictitious character — the creation of writer Stewart Kinross, who first introduced him in a short story called *Bradman Move Over*. Just as no anthology of the best writing on English cricket could ignore the hilarious account of a cricket match from A.G. Macdonnell's novel *England their England*, so no anthology of fine writing about New Zealand cricket would seem complete to me without the immortal Sid Smith. This is Kinross's second story about his schoolboy hero, *The Touch of Genius*.

It has been extremely gratifying to learn of the enthusiasm concerning Sid Smith and the pride New Zealanders everywhere are displaying in the prowess, no matter how belated its disclosure, of one of our greatest sportsmen. Youth must have its heroes, and it is in the hope that Sid Smith will grow in the hearts of a generation that hadn't the good fortune to witness his skill that I have been persuaded to give some further details of Sid Smith at his glowing best.

One of his most ardent fans put it to me in this way. When we recall Bradman, we remember the great innings at Headingley, Leeds, in 1937. Think of McCabe, and there's that magnificent 180 not out against Larwood and Jardine. Similar occasions marking the genius from the common man come to mind when we recall Ranji or Macartney, Martin Donnelly or Sutcliffe (whether Herbert or Bert); Jack Hobbs had his moments of genius too. Give us something the fan urged, that we can similarly treasure from Sid Smith's career.

Now it would be simple to detail a great innings from Sid Smith's bat, where four succeeded four until the return of the ball from the boundary became mere monotony; these occasions display mastery but perhaps scarcely genius, so I have rejected them all. In Sid Smith's career such an innings was too commonplace to be worthy of mention. Genius demands something different, something individually distinctive.

I could perhaps give you Sid Smith's magnificent performance against a team from one of the town schools in the summer of 1911. How the match had been arranged I don't know, but we found ourselves one afternoon at this other school where the local kids made, if I remember rightly, 65. Sid Smith took eight wickets. In reply we had overtaken their score with a wicket or two in hand, Sid Smith on 57 not out, and myself, in the team for my spin bowling, on 1 not out. It was at this stage I overheard the suggestion being made among the other team that there was to be a second innings. I remember the feeling of panic, the hollow churning of the stomach, when I caught the remark casually tossed from slip to point that the second innings would reverse the result. My dismay may be understood when I tell you that every one of our team had jobs to do at home, jobs like finding the cow up the road where it had been grazing all day and bringing it home to be milked, or delivering papers or milk or fruit or eggs, or chopping firewood, or feeding the hens and the pigs, or any one of a hundred other things. Because of these calls, each of our players on the completion of his innings had headed back in the direction of home. They had a long way to go and they had to be on their way. Great bowler as Sid Smith was, he could not be expected to dismiss this capable side so cheaply again with a total fielding side of about two.

No wonder I was panic-stricken at the probability of our being robbed of victory by a stratagem. As the field recovered the ball from his next boundary, I rushed up to Sid, told him what I had overheard, and poured forth my fears. I can still remember the deep hooded look that came to Sid Smith's eyes, the look of a Napoleon facing a possible Waterloo; and then the confident turn back to the wicket. How would Bradman have faced the situation? Or Hutton, Macartney, Dempster, any of the giants of the past? The next ball came down, a full toss about knee high on the leg side. I can still see Sid's spring, the flash of the bat, the tigerish ferocity of it, and there, before our eyes, the compo ball split into two hemispheres which bounded their divergent ways towards two separate parts of the surrounding gorse hedge boundary. That, of course, was the end of the match; for one ball was all that any side could afford in those days and the one belonging to our team was already on its way home.

'Didja really mean to bust the ball?' I asked Sid Smith excitedly as we started to trot the 8 miles or so homeward. But I remember he just smiled in a secretive way. Genius does not discuss its methods.

That, of course, was dramatic enough; but I think this next incident discloses Sid Smith at his immaculate best. I had been induced by my mother, shortly before, to resume my attendance at Sunday School by her stressing two matters — first, that the annual Sunday School picnic was almost due, and secondly, that the new minister who had come to guide our spiritual destinies was an Otago representative cricketer. This was my mother's claim for him, and looking back I am inclined to doubt its accuracy, but I accepted it then without question. When picnic day arrived and we repaired to McKay's paddock to enjoy the revelries, it was with some misgiving that Sid Smith, Spadger McGovern, the Wilson kids and I, among others, discovered that the Reverend MacNaught had planned a Fathers versus Sons cricket match. We watched with sinking hearts when he produced a sugar bag from which he drew forth a couple of bats, stumps, a scorebook, and, believe it or not, a tennis ball. There was no mistaking his meaning, for there it was in all its revolting, woolly grey softness. This beaming man of God, this so-called Otago representative in clerical clothing, expected us not only to play cricket with a doddering bunch of cripples like our parents, but he expected us to play it with a tennis ball. There was born in me at that moment a contempt for Otago cricket that has persisted to this day.

It was then that Sid Smith displayed his first masterstroke — the touch of supreme genius that makes Lilliputians of those about him and raises him for all time to an eminence with the truly great. For with a gesture almost imperial Sid Smith produced from his pocket a brand-new compo ball still in its tissue paper, with the gold lettering shining virgin bright. He tossed it to the Reverend MacNaught and in a tone of utter finality remarked, 'We'll play with this!', walked out on the paddock and proceeded to erect the stumps.

Don't ask me where the ball came from. It could have been an unreported birthday or Christmas present; he could have found it, borrowed it, stolen it. Sid Smith never explained. His genius was displayed in his having it at the right moment at the right place, and his contemptuous rejection of a tennis ball as a cricketing tool deserves to rank with Cromwell's 'Take away that bauble' on another great historical occasion.

I shall not attempt to describe in all its revolting horror the progress of that match. The fathers, led by the Reverend MacNaught, batted first, each of them displaying the same silly condescension that could be compared only with the simpering of an elderly elephant in love for the first time. I remember we boys bowled and fielded with a sort of sullen grimness, determined to see this sickening ordeal through to its loathsome end. Finally we were given our turn to bat, and you can imagine our feelings when, with Sid Smith opening, the Reverend MacNaught placed his field in a close circle round the batsman. Sid obviously could not believe his eyes when Mr Mitchell, our class teacher, stationed himself about 3 yards away at silly leg.

'Hey!' he said. 'You'll be killed there!'

All he got in reply was Mr Mitchell's toothy smile and I could see Sid shaking his head in puzzlement. The Reverend MacNaught then sent down the first ball and (I know you will hardly credit this) he bowled underarm! Merciful heaven, but it was a painful moment. I can remember lying in the grass on the boundary and feeling as uncomfortable as I had ever done in a life teeming with painful situations. Most of my companions turned their heads away, the degradation being impossible to contemplate, but I watched in fascinated horror. Sid Smith himself could not credit what he saw, and the ball went past without his making a stroke. Then, as he waited for the next ball, I saw him shrug his shoulders and knew he had reached a decision. The ball came down and he smashed it, hard and true, with all the force of his outraged youth behind it straight into the midriff of Mr Mitchell at silly leg.

Well, the match ended with that stroke. By the time the Reverend MacNaught had pumped the wind back into Mr Mitchell's lungs and had half dragged, half carried him to the shade of the oak tree where a fluster of mothers took over; by the time he had explained three times to Mrs Mitchell that he had really intended the match to be played with a tennis ball but had weakly allowed himself to be overruled — by the time all this had happened most of the fathers had disappeared with Mr McKay to inspect his new separator, a task that took quite some time and from which they returned wiping their moustaches and sucking peppermints. By that time also we boys had disappeared to consider the birds nesting in McKay's plantation.

That innings requires no further elaboration; it was complete in itself, a gem without flaw. It ended forthwith a situation that had become intolerable, and it ended it in a way that dispensed completely with discussion and argument.

Such was Sid Smith's genius. As a boy I often envied Sid his mastery: the sweetness of his cover drive, the dancing grace of his square cut, the majesty of his hook shot. All these were poetry. But of all his shots, the one that in my opinion so clearly marked his genius, the one the least envious of us would most have desired to emulate, was that magnificent pull that ended the match at the Sunday School picnic.

Stewart Kinross *Please to Remember* (1963)

THREE

LIKE WATCHING
PAINT DRY?

Some people dislike cricket. My brothers, who will happily spend hours watching yachts tack into the far distance, tell me cricket is boring. Nothing ever happens, they say. Perhaps they are not looking at the right moment, for it is an unwritten law of cricket-watching that, as soon as you turn your back to buy a hot-dog, either wickets will start to tumble or someone will hit a six onto the roof of the stand.

Cricket is full of incident. There have been unsavoury moments — such as the unfortunate day in 1981, when the Australian captain, Greg Chappell, was so overcome by the desire to win at all costs that he told his brother Trevor to bowl the last ball of an international one-day match underarm, to prevent the unlikely possibility of New Zealand's number 10 batsman, Brian McKechnie, hitting a six to win the game.

There have been terrifying moments too, although fortunately not many of them. The short-pitched delivery that Peter Lever bowled to New Zealand's number 11, Ewen Chatfield, during the 1974–75 series against England, had a consequence not easily forgotten. The ball ricocheted off Chatfield's bat handle and hit him so hard it caused a hairline fracture of the skull. The England captain at the time was Mike Denness and three years later, when he published his autobiography *I Declare,* he was still haunted by images of the distraught Lever, and of Chatfield lying on the ground while the England physiotherapist worked to save his life.

Some cricketing moments are heroic. During the 1996 World Cup there was no more moving contribution to New Zealand's cause than Chris Harris's 130 in the quarter-final. Sweat-stained and staggering with fatigue and dehydration in the Indian heat, he all but put New Zealand in a position to defeat the tournament favourites, Australia. Their greater experience and depth of resources saw them to victory but, as the Duke of Wellington observed about the battle of Waterloo, 'it was a damned near-run thing'.

Cricket has more than its fair share of humorous moments: of fielders going for the same catch and colliding with each other instead, or total break-downs in communication that result in two batsmen standing at the same end — one looking foolish and the other furious. The England leg-spinner of the 1920s, Ian Peebles, told this story about Roger Blunt, the New Zealand all-rounder.

His promising partnership with an Australian batsman, whose twang was as sharp as his late cut, came to a sadly premature end when he was run out by the length of the pitch. He suddenly took off all by himself and arrived at the further end to find his opposite number motionless and looking the other way.

'Why did you call me if you weren't coming?' asked the astonished runner.

'I didn't,' replied the other, also surprised.

'You said "right",' insisted Blunt.

'Naow,' replied his partner scornfully. 'I said "Wight".'

Ian Peebles *Talking of Cricket* (1953)

To say that cricket is never dull would be claiming too much. When the game is ambling to a draw and the players are doing the minimum required to get themselves through to stumps, then even the most ardent admirers of the sport can be forgiven a few yawns. But there is always another day and another game to look forward to, and each game holds the prospect of excitement. There are times, in cricket, when you cannot take your eyes off the action for a moment.

The New Zealanders beat Hampshire here this evening by seven wickets. That prosaic fact conceals the most spectacular piece of cricket I have had the pleasure and the thrill of watching for many a long day.

Hampshire won for themselves all honour and glory by batting nearly all through the day, and taking their 120 for 3 overnight to 409, the largest score made by any side against the New Zealanders in England so far. When they were out at last the clock showed a quarter to six, so that by taking the extra half-hour the New Zealanders had only 35 minutes in which to make 109.

Hadlee sent in Sutcliffe and Donnelly, and lucky is the captain who can call upon two such cricketers for such a task. These two left-handers trusted their eye with a sequence of glorious strokes which must have made Ransom and Shackleton despair of where to pitch the next ball.

The first over produced 11 runs and the following four, 11, 14, 13 and 10 respectively, before Sutcliffe was caught off the last ball of the fifth over for 46. The innings had then lasted 13 minutes. Of the 30 balls bowled he had received 20, and had hit a six over long-off, another over mid-wicket, a third over extra cover, and four fours, all brilliant and powerful hits that left the field standing.

The total then was 59. Smith heightened the drama by being yorked first ball by Shackleton, then Reid hit a few and snicked a few while Donnelly took charge. In the seventh over Reid was bowled, also by Shackleton (77–3–9), and in the ninth over Hampshire had their last chance when Donnelly gave a nasty running catch to long-on, but it was put on the floor.

Hadlee now was with him, running like a stag, so that Donnelly, having expended a great deal of energy, was utterly outpaced. From the start the New Zealanders had been running for everything. Together Donnelly and Hadlee saw the thing through comfortably, Donnelly bringing the scores level with a vast six to square-leg, and leaning elegantly on the next, which flew to long-on for a single and victory. The time taken was 28 minutes.

E.W. Swanton *Cricket from all Angles* (1962)

Scoring 109 runs in 28 minutes, as the New Zealand team did against Hampshire on that June day in 1949, requires both sides to contribute. In those 28 minutes, Swanton records, 'Hampshire bowled 11.5 overs. How foolish of them: they had only to have a few consultations, do up a couple of bootlaces, and practise one or two more little tricks, and they would have saved the day!' Victories, or even spectacular run feasts, do not necessarily make a match memorable. There are times when one team's dour struggle to stave off defeat by superior opposition can be totally absorbing. The New Zealand touring party to England in 1958 was frighteningly inexperienced. Take away Bert Sutcliffe and John Reid and they were almost sacrificial lambs against an England eleven bristling with talent: Cowdrey, May, Godfrey Evans, Fred Trueman, the consummate spinning duo of Lock and Laker and that obdurate all-rounder Trevor Bailey. 'The New Zealanders played as though they were overawed' wrote John Arlott. But at Leeds, on 8 July 1958, the final day of the third test, the team defied the odds and two 19-year-olds put up such an heroic resistance that they nearly saved the match.

A sparse crowd watched New Zealand fall far and sadly short of the 168 runs they wanted to avoid an innings defeat — yet, in doing so, challenge that very probability.

Sutcliffe was lbw to Lock's second ball of the day: 34 for 4: Trueman caught Reid in Laker's leg-trap: 42 for 5: watchers from London enquired as to trains from Leeds on which luncheon was served. In what everyone assumed to be a brief phase of the morning's play Playle, in the defensive manner of Cowdrey, advanced his left foot down the wicket and played closely inside the shelter of his pad, his left hand well forward to keep the blade of the bat safely behind the handle. At the other end, MacGibbon batted as if he were in New Zealand. He has the fundamental soundness of batting in him. He uses his unusual height — about 6 feet 6 inches — to get over the ball, does not play slavishly back or forward, and has obviously been brought up to chastise the bad ball through his two main punishing stokes — the hook and the off-drive. From time to time, he brought these two strokes into effect and, when he hit Laker to leg for two, the New Zealand score rose to 50: at this point Playle had been in an hour and still had not scored. Lock and Laker changed ends but, for once, even that did not produce a wicket. MacGibbon, batting with good sense and good humour, made 39 — the highest individual score for New Zealand so far in this rubber — and, with Playle, had more than doubled the score when, just before lunch, he left unplayed a ball from Lock he judged to be passing outside the leg stump; in fact, it straightened and MacGibbon was lbw: 88 for 6. By lunch, Playle had been in since three minutes after the start and had scored 2: Sparling had taken MacGibbon's place.

For a few minutes after lunch the two young batsmen were not quite certain of themselves. Playle's first false stroke of the day — a hasty edge through the slips off Lock — went for four and carried the New Zealand score to 100. Thereat, as if to convince someone — perhaps himself — of his confidence, Playle threw his left foot forward and, from a high back-lift, let the bat flow through its full swing in a cover-drive of utter grace, technically perfect and so exactly timed that the field could only stand and watch it. Lock applauded the stroke, looked with puzzlement at its maker and then, snatching the ball out of the air as it was thrown back to him, marched belligerently back to bowl again. He found Playle, however, entrenched in his former mood, playing with the shallow pendulum of a very straight bat, refusing all temptation; batting with both eyes fixed on the ball but his mind, apparently, on eternity.

May took the new ball: Trueman, Loader and Bailey used it, and still the two junior New Zealanders batted on, leaving anything they might unplayed, otherwise defending with passive bats, taking runs only when the defensive stroke carried the ball clear of the close field on to turf which had become faster as it dried out. Three o'clock came and then a quarter-past: half-past: half the day's play was gone and only three New Zealand wickets had fallen; only one — MacGibbon's — in the last three hours. Each of the five English bowlers had been thrown against Playle and Sparling: the spinners had changed ends: the new ball had come, the new ball had lost its shine; the spinners had come back: and still neither batsmen had given a ghost of a chance, despite the ring of fieldsmen close up to their bats. The ball still turned, but only slowly — and a pitch always seems to grow easier when the bowlers tire and lack the stimulus of success. There was no need to make strokes or runs: runs, indeed, were useless to New Zealand now, with little more than two and a half hours until the end of the match. Any risk taken in an attempt to score endangered the batsmen's true and only objective — to save the game. To deny England victory was all that could be done: for the first time in the day that hitherto theoretical eventuality became cricketing possibility. It may have been in Playle's mind, as an objective — distant but worth striving for — when he first came to the wicket. Now, clearly, he had planted it in the minds of the English players. Playle, they had now to recognise, had batted already, without mistake, for more than three hours — longer than the time remaining to the end of the match.

A new — half-irritated — tension could be sensed as the ball, short or full, fast, medium or slow, thumped dishearteningly against two straight and patient bats or on the pads beside them: artifices were frustrated by unremitting concentration; urgent certainty had given way to patient plugging away on England's part. Laker now bowled from the Kirstall Lane end where Lock had been: Playle again leant forward in the stroke now implanted in the fielders' minds, poised, wary, playing for the off-break — but the ball did not turn: if anything, it ran on, and it flicked the off-bail. Playle had batted three and a quarter hours for 18 runs. In his third test match — and only the twenty-fifth first-class game of his entire career! — he had come nearer to saving a lost match than anyone since England prevented Australia from winning at Lord's in 1953. That, however, was a joint effort, between Compton — in the crucial early stages — Watson and Bailey. Playle had Sparling with him for less than half his innings which, as a single defensive effort, falls little short of Bruce Mitchell's resistance at the oval in 1947. It may yet prove to have been the first major test innings of a player who eventually will take a place among the great batsmen of the world. Admittedly, with the glorious exception of that single cover-drive, it was virtually strokeless, but strokes were not called for — rather the reverse. It has received little recognition. Critics are but human; it is possible that some of them were disappointed that a whole string of trains due to arrive in London at convenient hours, should have pulled out of Leeds without them while Playle prolonged the game as far beyond their expectations as those of the English team.

John Arlott *John Arlott's Cricket Journal* (1958)

In the centenary year of 1995, the New Zealand men's cricket team became adept at snatching defeat from the jaws of victory as the players lost the self-belief so evident during the highly successful 1980s. Perhaps the problem was that the achievements of the previous decade had given them unreal expectations. They forgot that their predecessors' self-belief had been backed up with a fighting spirit learned from past generations of New Zealand cricketers, who had battled superior forces with such gritty determination that they sometimes surprised the world. If ever a match pointed the way towards New Zealand's glorious years in the 1980s, it was the first test against England at Trent Bridge in June 1973.

New Zealand had played test cricket against England for 42 years but not a single test match had been won. They could find good cricketers but never field a strong enough eleven to challenge England. Such, at any rate, was the acccepted doctrine when the seventh New Zealand team to meet England on their own territory landed in 1973.

Not even the craggy features of captain Bevan Congdon, whose deadpan and disapproving expression recalled a Scottish presbyterian minister in a gloomy mood on a wet Sunday afternoon, could turn this Kiwi team into a threatening unit. A man of stubborn intent, he was respected by colleagues as a cricketer rather than beloved as a leader. As the teams came to Trent Bridge for the first test, there had already been murmurings of discontent at his aloof attitudes and cautious tactics. He had much to do to convince his team of his standing.

At first things went well. Batting first on a hot, sunny day England slipped from 92 without loss to 191 for 9 as the New Zealand bowlers plugged away, bowling line and length to an unrelentingly defensive field. Only a late flurry from Alan Knott and Norman Gifford took England to 250.

On the second morning the air was heavy as New Zealand were hustled out for 97. Humiliation, ever a threat to Kiwi cricketers of this era, was once more in prospect.

Fighting back, New Zealand quickly restored the balance to the game by reducing England to 24 for 4, but once more the door was to be closed, as Amiss and Greig, the careworn and the cavalier, added 210, allowing Illingworth to declare 478 runs in front. Only the wildest New Zealand optimist at Trent Bridge was forecasting anything more than 200 second time around.

When Turner and John Parker were brushed aside with only 16 upon the board everyone's worst fears appeared merely to await their confirmation. With over an hour left for play that Saturday night and with his hopes in tatters, Congdon took guard and prepared to face Snow and Arnold. With runs to spare Illingworth had set an aggressive field and Congdon was quickly able to open his account and take ten off an over from Snow. And then, as if his load were not already enough, he mishooked Snow and edged the ball into his face, which was bruised, swollen and cut.

Congdon's face was still in disorder as play resumed on the Monday morning. Within 18 minutes his team was in greater disorder still, for at 68, Hastings fell to Arnold. Mark Burgess entered and at once began to play his cultured shots. Moving impassively Congdon reached his 50 in 106 minutes but lost Burgess for 26 at 130. At lunch New Zealand were 146 for 4 with Vic Pollard hanging on grimly, and it was not until after the break that this pair began to take charge. As, with watchful defence and occasional aggressive shots, they built their partnership, so a change came over the game, a change detectable in the hushed pressbox and fascinated crowd, for both men appeared impregnable and, quite suddenly, England were in a contest.

Between lunch and tea 87 runs were added taking New Zealand to 233 for 4, a marvellous fightback but still a hopeless position. Already Congdon had kept England at bay for five hours, hours during which the merest slip on his part would have meant inevitable defeat. Upon his shoulders had rested not merely this game but the very reputation of New Zealand cricket. At last, with the bowlers losing control, Congdon and Pollard were able to advance with fierce cuts, pulls and drives as the game slowly turned. Congdon had reached his hundred after 220 minutes of hard-headed and practical batting, and now he was surging on, with Pollard still resolute in support.

As the close approached, and Pollard passed his 50 after 203 minutes at the crease, Congdon continued as if nothing on earth could shift him, for he habitually hid his emotions and here he was disguising that dangerous combination, exhilaration and exhaustion. Finally, and even surprisingly, Arnold threaded a ball through his defences and with only 15 minutes left to play, he was out.

New Zealand were 307 for 5. Congdon had scored 176 runs in 412 minutes and hit 19 boundaries. He left to a warm, even moving ovation. It had been an innings born in despair which died in hope, an innings played against overwhelming odds on behalf of a weak team in a dreadful state against a formidable enemy. It had been an innings of great skill and, most importantly, immense psychological courage.

Nor did its significance end with that shattering of stumps by Arnold, for Congdon had filled the Kiwis' hearts with fight. From 317 for 5 overnight Pollard and Wadsworth took the score to 402, just 72 short of victory. At lunch, New Zealand needed 70 with four wickets left.

To his bitter disappointment Pollard departed leg before after lunch and, breathing defiance to the end, the Kiwis' heroic struggle fell 39 runs short of the target. Thoroughly inspired, New Zealand outplayed England in the following drawn test at Lord's.

Congdon's innings showed New Zealanders what could be done, and helped to build a resistance and a spirit within New Zealand cricket which was to take them from the bottom rung of the test cricket ladder nearly to its top.

Peter Roebuck *Great Innings* (1989)

Some of the most exciting moments in cricket come when a player takes a game by the scruff of the neck and gives it a good shaking. J.R. Reid was always liable to produce something special. The record-breaking feat he describes in this passage was not eclipsed until 1995.

Although I have always enjoyed following what the better cricket writers have to say about a game, I cannot claim to have read the full works of Mr Neville Cardus a dozen times and more. I don't look, particularly, for the classical allusion or colourful imagery. But I confess I was really startled to see the heading on an article about me which appeared in an English publication designed to appeal to children — particularly, perhaps, to those who have never heard of Cardus. The heading described me as *The Kiwi King of Slog*. While sympathising with the newspaper workers who have to write headings which fit into small spaces, this seemed to me to be just a little forced, a little too colourful, and not, really, much of a contribution to the literature of cricket.

I suppose really I must have been a bit embarrassed by it. I have had to abdicate too often to be a really successful king! But I have, for all that, always enjoyed trying to get on top of the opposing bowling. My most successful innings in that particular direction was at the Basin Reserve in January 1963 when Wellington was playing Northern Districts. In that innings I made the top score of my career, 296, and I set a world record by hitting 15 sixes. What does it feel like to set a world record? I really don't know. I hadn't the slightest idea, until I saw the paper next morning, that the previous record, shared by Richie Benaud, Charles Barnett, and the Indian C.K. Nayudu, had been 11 sixes in an innings. At the risk of sounding immodest, I think that when a batsman is in the form I found that day at the Basin, he is capable of making the opposing bowlers look pretty ordinary. But after this innings was over, a typical New Zealand cricketing reaction was to be heard — it was a spectacular innings, all right, but the bowling had been terribly weak. My own innings, and this match, put aside for a moment — it is a pity that so many New Zealand cricket followers take that line. They are always prepared to believe that if any New Zealand player achieves something out of the ordinary, it must be because the other players are no good. That attitude doesn't help our cricketers win the confidence they need.

In this particular instance, I don't think that Northern Districts had a weak bowling side. It just happened to be my day. Northern Districts, that season, had started its campaign by taking first-innings points from Auckland. It had then beaten Otago outright, and gone down to Wanganui to defeat Central

Districts by the comfortable margin of five wickets, before moving on to Wellington. Don Clarke, although much more distinguished in another sphere of sporting activity, was a good, lively fast-medium bowler — sufficiently good and sufficiently lively to have taken, at Wanganui, eight Central Districts wickets for 37 in the second innings of the match. Also in the side were Gren Alabaster, who had taken five wickets at moderate cost, P.H. Barton, who had taken 4 for 48 in the first innings of the shield series, useful performers such as Peter McGregor and Terry Shaw, and the outstanding off-spinner of recent shield series, Tom Puna, who had had a match analysis of 7 for 70 against Otago and 6 for 68 against Central Districts…

The sixes at the Basin came from Puna (two), Alabaster, Clarke and Barton (three each) and Shaw (four). When it was done, one of the statisticians gave me a table which explains, better than words, the reaction of a fielding team to a batsman who is thoroughly on top. At first, I was able to keep the ball down, and in making my first 50 in 67 minutes, I hit 11 fours and no sixes at all. But as my innings progressed, the field settings became deeper and deeper and it never really occurred to me, because I felt so confident, to pick up the singles. I felt it was then a matter of hitting over the top. My second 50, in 32 minutes, had five fours and three sixes. The third 50 was in 35 minutes, with six fours and three sixes, and then there was a bit of a lull. I went from 150 to 200 in 33 minutes, hitting eight fours. From 200 to 250, in 28 minutes, I had four fours and four sixes, and in the last stage of the innings, with just about everyone on the boundary, I made 46 in 25 minutes, with only one four but five sixes.

The scoring board at the Basin is not the most modern of its kind, but the boys there were kept very busy shinning up the ladders to put up the numbers, and they did remarkably well. They certainly let me know that I was nearly at 300, a score I had never achieved. I suppose I could and should have — from my own personal point of view — picked up the last few quietly, but I got out, at 296, trying to hit another six. I tried to put one over long-on but got an inside edge and was taken on the mid-wicket boundary.

And although I had hit 50 boundaries for 230 of my runs, there was a rather typical comment from one or two businessmen who arrived late at the ground. They had just sat down when I was dismissed. 'Just like Reid,' said one of them. 'Bull at a gate — and out he goes.'

J.R. Reid *A Million Miles of Cricket* (1966)

Another who could turn a match was Richard Hadlee. In November 1985 he accomplished amazing feats against Australia at the 'Gabba ground in Brisbane. The supporting cast, featuring Martin Crowe and another John Reid — J.F. rather than J.R. — was superb, too, and the result was an innings victory to a team that had been written off by the Australian commentators before play began.

I'd never known a test when we had prepared so thoroughly and planned so meticulously, and yet there was nothing in the early stages of the tour which suggested this would be an extraordinary match. We'd never won a test in Australia and there wasn't any hint we were about to alter history; certainly we hadn't been overwhelmingly dominant in the state matches against South Australia and Queensland.

But there was a dream-like quality about the first morning of the match. The atmospheric conditions were clammy, humid and there was low cloud and the threat of showers; my fingers were twitching. The toss was another triumph. Jeremy Coney called correctly and in no time it was all happening.

South African-born Kepler Wessels took strike and instantly scored a single…which offered me the attractive prospect of bowling to Australia's happy hooker, Andrew Hilditch. Now, Hilditch was as partial to the hook shot as I used to be to chocolate fish, so it was only natural we would exploit his partiality — and weakness — for one of the riskier shots in the game. As it happened, we never really had time to give him the bait and set the trap; he simply obliged without any prompting, whipping a slightly shorter delivery to fine-leg where Charlie Chatfield held the catch above his head. Only five balls into the test and we were away. One wicket, especially an early one, doesn't necessarily determine the course of a match — but in this case we felt it would.

Everything was humming from the outset. The ball was going through well — bouncing, seaming and swinging. I had a perfect ball, a nice dark one which felt good in my hand and, with Chatfield operating from the other end, the Australian batsmen were uncomfortable, not able to cope with the moving ball for a long period. Despite such psychological ascendancy, it took us time to gain more statistical success; not until just before lunch did I lure David Boon to chase a wider delivery and offer Coney's sure hands the kind of morsel they love at second slip.

The real bonus came after lunch. My first ball was a loosener, a delivery which showed all the signs of a player who might have had a little too much to eat at the break. For reasons known only to him, Allan Border was drawn to this wide offering when he might well have let it sail through to the 'keeper. He launched into a cracking cover drive, but hit it aerially and precisely to Bruce Edgar at cover. Soon after, 72 for 3 became 82 for 4 when I also had Greg Ritchie's wicket. Then, nicely on cue, the light faded shortly after the tea break, the day ending prematurely with Australia 146 for 4. It was a promising position for us, although not commanding, especially with Wessels in on 69 and Wayne Phillips on 25.

However, the abbreviated day benefited us, and certainly me. It meant I returned for the second day as fresh as I'd been at the start of the first. It was like starting a new test match; the ball still had sufficient shine on it and the pitch and weather conditions were again in our favour. What followed in the next hour would have been unbelievable, except that I was there taking part in some of the most sensational scenes I've witnessed in my career. We'd gained confidence from our deeds on the opeining day without quite taking a stranglehold on the match. Now we did.

It was incredible to think Australia, within an hour of the second day starting, was all out for 179. It was positively out of this world to find I'd taken nine wickets myself and had a part in all ten dismissals by taking a catch from Geoff Lawson to give my Canterbury team-mate Vaughan Brown his first test wicket, and, as it happens, his only one. There I was so close to all ten, within reach of emulating Jim Laker's 10 for 53 against Australia at Old Trafford in 1956. This was a freak happening. I swear the ball talked throughout that test innings; I've never seen a ball behave and respond the way that one did. It'd be trite to say it, but that is by far the best bowling performance I've achieved. It would have to be, wouldn't it? You dream of figures like this…23.4 overs, 4 maidens, 52 runs, 9 wickets. But you never expect them to happen, and definitely not in a test…

Good as the figures were, they wouldn't have meant half as much if they hadn't catapulted New Zealand to a test win. I revel in personal success but always I want such feats to lead to the grander prize of test victories and series wins. This time, the theme of perfection was maintained throughout. Our specialist batsmen performed magnificently, led by Martin Crowe's splendid 188 and John Reid's 108 as they put on 224 for a New Zealand third-wicket record (bettered in 1986–87 by John Wright and Crowe against the West Indies in Wellington). For the best part of two days we made Australia suffer and, in gathering gloom, I had the added satisfaction of making 54 — the 50 off only 41 balls — as we went on to 553 for 7 declared, New Zealand's highest total in a test.

Day four…two days left to bowl Australia out, the home side trailing by 374 runs. What a position to be in! With play beginning at 10.30 (to compensate for Brisbane's poor twilight), we immediately had the Australian second innings teetering — and this time Chatfield was the destroyer, not Hadlee. First Wessels was out for three and then Boon for one. Play was halted at 11.00 to mark Remembrance Day by a minute's silence. We stood in a huddle and I have to admit a lack of courtesy by failing to honour the period of silence…the ball lay on the ground in the middle, I would be bowling to Hilditch when play resumed and I said: 'Think Hilditch, think bouncer, think hook shot, think catch, think out!'

This time we brought our plan into play and, just as unbelievably as the first innings, Hilditch couldn't help himself. I fed him a short delivery, he impulsively hooked and there was Chatfield doing the business again — from the very first ball after the break! It showed gross irresponsibility and indiscipline on Hilditch's part as Australia plunged to 16 for 3. The test was definitely ours. It was only a matter of time.

Australia slipped further to 67 for 5 before Border found an ally in Matthews. They batted on and on, first Matthews going through to his maiden test hundred — and going way over the top when he celebrated it — and then Border to his fifteenth. We were getting a bit weary, jaded and had some moments of reservation but, just before stumps, Coney took the new ball for me to have a desperate crack. It worked. Minutes into my spell Matthews was gone, caught by Coney for 115 and we knew the rest would be academic.

From 266 for 6, Australia was all out for 333 on the fifth day and again I had five wickets in an innings — 6 for 71 off 28.5 overs — and match figures of 15 for 123. More statistical delight — my best match figures in first-class cricket and comfortably the best in New Zealand's test history (beating the 11 I'd taken against India in 1975–76 and the West Indies in 1979–80). And the feat of taking nine wickets in an innnings and scoring a 50 in the same match was unique in test cricket! That was incidental. At last New Zealand had won a test in Australia, and won it stylishly and emphatically, as the winning margin of an innings and 41 runs would suggest. It's the most perfect match I've played in, quite beyond comparison.

Richard Hadlee with Richard Becht **Rhythm and Swing** (1989)

Where were you on 17 February 1973? The question defines a generation — it is New Zealand's cricketing equivalent of 'where were you when President Kennedy was assassinated?' It was Rodney Redmond's day and those who were at Eden Park, or heard the radio commentary, know that it was the stuff of which legends are made.

The third test against Pakistan in the 1972–73 season would have been striking enough without Redmond's contribution. The visitors made 402 in their first innings, with Majid Khan scoring a century, and then Intikhab Alam mesmerised New Zealand to take six wickets, before Brian Hastings and Richard Collinge chipped in to bring the scores level. Their 151 for the tenth wicket broke a test record that had stood for 69 years. Yet it was Redmond — a 'tall left-hander with the looks of a Greek god' — who set the game afire with his debut test match innings.

He started none to well against the faster bowlers, sometimes stranded by the bouncers and plainly ill at ease at the sharpness of Saleem's swing. Sensibly Redmond did the thing he does best — playing strokes. Out flowed the shots, cuts and pulls, gorgeous drives through cover or lofted toward mid-on. Khan bowled his first five balls — Redmond hit them to the fence at long off, third man, long on, square leg and extra cover. He raced from 44 to 86 by the simple, dazzling process of hitting ten fours and two singles.

Khan lasted only three overs for 30 of these runs, and even Intikhab was treated with little respect. However, the stern test was still to come. For all Turner's cool, steadying influence at the other end, Redmond's batting took on a slightly frenetic touch. At 89 he slashed at Intikhab, mishit, and as the chance lobbed gently up, Intikhab and Mustaq seemed to indicate 'after you' before Mustaq darted in a fraction too late. The next ball was crashed away for four, a misfield brought two, a soaring hit to long on another two, and another wallop to leg would have brought four had not Asif Iqbal spurted along the fence and cut it to two.

Several hundred spectators, thinking he had reached his century with a boundary, raced out and poor Redmond had to be freed from the clamouring mob. The tension was gripping, the 14,000 crowd deathly silent as Intikhab bowled the next ball, and the roar and the mob crashed forward again as Redmond cracked the ball to the extra cover fence. Visibly affected by the tumult, he had time for only one more boundary before he sliced a drive and Mushtaq held the catch.

The statistics give some hint of Redmond's incredible innings. He scored his century in 196 minutes from only 110 balls. Altogether he batted 145 minutes, hit 20 fours and a five. His 107 came from only 38 scoring shots.

But what the statistics can never tell is the drama, the breath-taking tension, the audacity of an innings that will remain a piece of Eden Park history. For Redmond came on the scene like a comet — and he may well remain as a star.

D.J. Cameron 'The Test with Everything', **New Zealand Herald** 19 February 1973

That was Redmond's finest hour. Not long afterwards he apparently suffered eye problems and drifted out of the game, but at least he had given himself and New Zealand cricket something to remember. There are certain events that it would be almost kinder to forget — except that they are part of our cricketing history and cannot be ignored. Take the summer of 1954–55, for example, when New Zealand set an all-time record for low scores, culminating in what is still the worst total ever made in a test match innings. It happened at Eden Park, against an England team which had just beaten Australia comprehensively to retain the Ashes, and the irony was that, at one stage, New Zealand had the chance to force a victory. Bert Sutcliffe, who was in the team that day, remembered the game being 'a fearful struggle for runs', right from the opening overs.

I felt in fine form at that time, but just before lunch on the first day I lost my concentration, had a go at Wardle, and got out for 49. In the afternoon John Reid batted superbly for 73, but our day brought us only 199 for 8, and next morning we finished with 200. This looked much too modest a score to contain England's batting, but New Zealand in the field was a much more forthright team than New Zealand batting. Before an attendance of about 30,000, quite remarkable by New Zealand standards, we kept England down to 148 for 4 at the close of a day in which rain cost a little time. On the third morning our bowlers were magnificent and Reid in the close leg-side position took two brilliant catches. It was then I saw Hutton score what I consider was the most selfish half-century I have watched from an international. His side was in trouble, for everyone, even our opponents and their pressmen, felt at that stage that New Zealand had a distinct chance of winning. But Hutton, batting at number five, was content to push for a single and leave most of the over to others low on the batting list. It seemed to me to be a clear case of an England captain shelving responsibility. The visitors were 164 for 7, 199 for 8, — and it was Frank Tyson who helped them to a lead of 46; it did not seem nearly enough for safety. Alex Moir, spinning cleverly, and a determined John Hayes took most of the wickets, but Reid and Cave yielded no more than a run an over.

Our own Waterloo began in mid-afternoon, and it lasted a matter of 27 overs. I still cannot fully explain how we were out for 26. Bad batting, of course. Good bowling, undoubtedly. Lack of resolution, almost certainly. And perhaps the intensity of the struggle earlier had taken something out of our rather inexperienced and diffident batsmen. It really was an extraordinary affair. My score of 11 was easily top. I was fifth out, at 14, taking a swing at Wardle. I went back, had a quick shower, and as I emerged from the dressing-room the last of our batsmen were coming in.

A Christchurch friend had an even worse experience. Hearing on the radio that England was struggling, he dropped all ideas of work and hurried to catch a plane for Auckland. At that time the New Zealand internal service was operated with DC3s, fine aircraft, but not swift by more recent standards. This traveller, a very keen cricketer, started his flight about the time we started our innings. The pilot was good enough to pass back messages to him, giving him the score at frequent intervals. Long before he had covered the 500-odd miles to Auckland, the game was over.

It seemed hardly fair, in a way, that we should have been so humiliated after putting up so stout-hearted a performance for two and a half days. However, it had to be remembered that the Australian batting had been cut into pieces almost as small. This game was the only one I can remember playing in where a player has collected a royal pair. Colquhoun was caught in the same position, from the same bowler, first ball in each innings.

All out, 26. Incredible. But as one of our well-wishers said, all the runs came from the bat!

Bert Sutcliffe *Between Overs* (1963)

According to R.T. Brittenden, in his *The Finest Years of New Zealand Cricket*, a prominent Wellington businessman once declared that New Zealand cricketers should have their passports withdrawn, to stop them lowering the country's prestige overseas with their seemingly inevitable defeats. Times change. By the 1970s New Zealand were no longer the easy-beats of world cricket but an often formidable side, especially on home territory.

As the New Zealanders sat down to lunch on 14 February, the fourth day of this tense, low-scoring, blustery test, they could season the cold meat and salad with some pleasant arithmetic. New Zealand, 13 runs ahead on the first innings — 228 to 215 — had reached 75 for the loss of Robert Anderson's wicket.

There were ten hours to play and New Zealand, with a total lead of 88, were handily placed. Another solid afternoon and New Zealand could end the day a shade over 200 to the good and probably with enough wickets in hand to organise a declaration on the fifth morning, perhaps asking England to score 250 in five hours. The pitch was already awkward, with an erratic bounce, and the bowlers of both sides had been allowed to scrape holes in it close enough to the line of the stumps to worry the batsmen.

It was a pleasant prospect. New Zealand were in a position from which they hardly could lose, and might even win on the last afternoon. It was, then, a pleasant lunch.

Within an hour that same lunch was sitting heavily in the pits of New Zealand stomachs. Bob Willis, the tousel-haired England fast bowler, came roaring downwind like a ferocious lion. In his first 31 balls after lunch Willis had John Wright out at 82, Geoff Howarth and Bevan Congdon at 93 and John Parker at 98 — all caught as the ball careered madly off the worn pitch. At 99 Ian Botham had Mark Burgess caught, with a top edge from a hopeful hook. At 104 Willis struck again, with Richard Hadlee caught — giving the England giant five wickets for 15 from 43 balls.

As a rather more subtle afterthought Mike Hendrick had Warren Lees lbw at 116 for 8 — after the little wicketkeeper had made one of the few genuine strokes of the afternoon with a cover drive for four. At 123 Hendrick and Ian Botham finished off the innings.

In two disastrous hours New Zealand had lost nine wickets for 48 runs, and England needed only 137 in eight hours to win. It seemed the cruellest luck for the New Zealanders, as they cast away all the advantage so dearly won by the batting of Wright and Congdon in the first innings, and the great-hearted bowling of Collinge and Richard Hadlee which had held England to such a modest score, even while conceding 77 painstaking runs to Geoff Boycott.

Once again the rare prize of a first victory over England seemed to have been snatched away from New Zealand.

The few thousand despondent New Zealanders were settling into their seats as Richard Hadlee bowled his first over, hurtling in from the end from which Willis had done so much damage. Collinge, into the breeze from the other end, seemed merely an interlude, for he was slower than Hadlee and not liable to get the ball to fly up into the batsmen's ribs.

Collinge wheeled down three without causing Boycott any concern. The fourth was of fuller length and Boycott decided that it could be hit very firmly between mid-wicket and mid-on. It was a brave shot for any opening batsman so early in an innings. For Boycott it was a strange stroke, quite out of character with his riskless batting in the first innings, when for 442 minutes he had laboured for his 77, all the time giving the impression that he was the umbrella under which his other batsmen — many of them out of form or not of true test quality — could shelter.

Perhaps, too, Boycott decided that his slow grind for runs in the first innings should be succeeded by a more positive attitude in pursuing such a modest winning target. Two or three solidly hit boundaries at the start might well deflate the New Zealand bowlers and encourage his own batsmen.

So Boycott launched into the shot but had to hit slightly across the line, so much so that his back foot kicked up off the ground. In that slight across-the-line movement Boycott misjudged the line of the ball, it was through him and ripped into the middle and off stumps.

Boycott out for one, England only two — the whole ground erupted and on the field the New Zealanders threw off the depression which had gathered about them between lunch and tea. The great man was gone, the batsman who had foiled them for over seven hours in the first innings. Another wicket and perhaps England might tremble. It came in Collinge's next over. The ball lifted quickly, Geoff Miller jabbed and at gully Anderson had the catch. Two for eight runs, and now Richard Hadlee was like a tiger let loose from his cage. He bowled a murderous ball at Brian Rose, lifting and coming into the left-hander, who had no chance of a stroke and had to take the ball on his elbow. Rose crumpled with the pain, he had no feeling in the arm, he had to go off.

But Collinge was not done. In his next over he managed an inswinger of full pitch. Derek Randall shuffled across and looked unhappy when Collinge's triumphant appeal for lbw was granted. It was a magnificent ball for an out-of-form batsman so early in his innings and, as the television replays showed later, a very good umpiring decision.

Now, at 18 for 3 — Collinge all three for nine runs from 17 balls — it was Richard Hadlee's turn. Graham Roope, who had played and missed so much in the first innings, this time got an early edge, Lees had the catch and England were 18 for 4, and perhaps 5, for the early reports were that Rose's elbow might have been broken.

Botham, a brash young man, decided that bold methods were the best. Whenever Hadlee dropped short, Botham hooked. He scored three fours and the score jumped from 18 to 38. But when Botham hooked he hit in the air. It took Burgess a long time to arrange a fieldsman in the appropriate place, but inevitably Botham hooked in the air and at backward square Stephen Boock held the catch — 38 for 5.

Then came one of those bonuses which often go to teams on the rampage. Chris Old squeezed a ball from Hadlee square and as Boock pursued it Bob Taylor went for the single. In a blur of movement Boock fielded, turned and threw in the same sweep, and hit the stumps from side-on to run Taylor out. Phil Edmonds, looking poised, worked the score into the fifties, but at 53 Hadlee had Old lbw and Hendrick caught, leaving Edmonds and Willis together.

The match would have ended then had another wicket fallen, for Rose was in no condition to bat, but England finished out the day at 53 for 8 — still wanting 84 runs, a less likely mission than the two wickets New Zealand required.

All New Zealand prayed that evening that the Welligton weather, never the most predicatable quantity, would not turn sour and wash out the New Zealand victory the next day.

Soon after breakfast the next morning all the fears seemed to haunt New Zealand. Light, drizzling rain set in — wafted along by a northerly breeze. The covers stayed on and although Wellingtonians insisted that the wind would soon blow the rain away, the few hundred people at the Basin Reserve moped sombrely about.

For once the Wellingtonians were right. The rain did go away and, 40 minutes after the scheduled start, the New Zealanders went out for the final act. It had a quiet opening, Dayle Hadlee bowling one over so Richard Hadlee could change to bowl downwind from the north. There was a trickle of runs, and Hadlee was warned for bowling a bouncer at Edmonds, who qualified as a 'non-recognised batsman'. The score edged into the sixties and it took 40 minutes for the New Zealanders to make the final breakthrough. Edmonds got an edge to the seventh ball of Hadlee's third over and Parker had the catch at first slip. A single to Rose, a maiden to Collinge, Willis off to square leg to complain about a flier from Hadlee and then the end — Willis jabbing at Hadlee and at gully Howarth swooping down, taking the ball in one hand and then holding it aloft in triumph.

Then everone went mad. The champagne bottles were open long before Hadlee, 6 for 26, and Collinge, 3 for 35, led the jubilant New Zealanders from the field and into the history books.

Don Cameron *Memorable Moments in New Zealand Sport* (1979)

New Zealand had won tests before that 1978 victory over England, and would win others in the future, yet that particular match seemed to create an unusual surge of excitement. For a few days cricket became more than a game — it seemed to sum up the spirit of a nation.

During the 1992 World Cup it again captured the imagination of the country. New Zealand, despised and demoralised just a few weeks before the tournament started, became giant-killers. Soon, even those who had never shown an interest in the game were talking enthusiastically about cricket. It all began with a victory over Australia on 22 February, which left writers from across the Tasman in a state of bewildered admiration.

Stepping into the cacophony at Eden Park for the opening World Cup match between the tournament's joint hosts was like stepping into the bird enclosure at a zoo. As the Australians discovered, that can be a messy business.

Thirty-five thousand cheap party hooters — more than one per head — were shipped in from China and distributed free for the occasion. The people of Auckland blew with gusto as New Zealand, previously thought to be as capable of flight as the dodo, soared into the unexpected and descended on Australia from a great height.

The effect on the ears, if you closed your eyes, was that of a mass strangulation of ducks. The effect on the World Cup was to provide it with the spiciest opening imaginable.

Australia was the raging tournament favourite; New Zealand, consensus had it, a basket case.

The upset victory was designed and constructed by Martin Crowe, who dominated the match with his batting and unorthodox captaincy. He won an important toss and batted when the wicket was at its best, hit an exquisite unbeaten century to steer New Zealand to 6 for 248, and then defended the total with tactics that were radical for their ultra-defensiveness.

His bravest move was to open the bowling at the terrace end with the part-time off-spin of Dipak Patel, which sent a murmur through the crowd. He also adopted a revolving door policy with his anonymous band of medium-pacers, alternating them so often that he might as well have put stockings over their heads to prevent the batsmen from recognising them and getting into rhythm. Chris Harris, for example, bowled his 7.1 overs in four spells.

The strapping Chris Cairns bowled four expensive overs and was dispensed with on the grounds that his pace and waywardness gave the Australian batsmen something to work with. The policy of the rest seemed to be to land the ball as softly as a powder puff on a woman's cheek.

'They've done the dirty on us again,' [Alan] Border said afterwards, albeit with a smile. The loss confirmed his worst fears that the opening match of Australia's World Cup defence was its most dangerous. 'As soon as Australia hit New Zealand soil [the New Zealanders] lift 50 per cent. I've seen it in rugby and I've seen it in cricket,' he said.

Australia did not adjust well to the conditions. On a wicket that had reasonable pace to start with but grew increasingly sluggish as the day progressed, they bowled too short, particularly to Crowe.

Crowe is one of the most classical and effective pullers in the game. Of his 11 boundaries, seven were the result of pull shots, some of them so savage that a fieldsman standing within 5 metres of the boundary had no hope of intercepting them.

Aside from three dropped catches — including a sitter by Tom Moody at first slip to reprieve Rod Latham — the luck seemed to run with the New Zealand batsmen. Perhaps a more logical explanation was that Australia had trouble with the strange angles and short boundaries created by Eden Park's bizarre shape. Border admitted afterwards that whenever he looked round the warped septagonal field his fielders seemed to be in the wrong place.

The essential difference between the sides was that while New Zealand, and Ken Rutherford in particular, batted cleverly around Martin Crowe, Australia's century-maker, David Boon, played the role of a lone and defiant standard-bearer for much of his innings.

Dean Jones was unlucky to be given run out by Pakistani umpire Khizar Hayat (just as New Zealand's Jones, Andrew, was unfortunate to be adjudged lbw by the same umpire earlier in the day). But after Dean Jones went, three Australian wickets fell in quick succession in a more culpable fashion.

Border presented his wicket to Patel, holing out to deep square leg from only his eleventh delivery; Tom Moody thought he was back in Perth, completing his shot before the ball had arrived and popping up a diving return catch for Latham; and Mark Waugh persisted with his habit of playing across the line to be lbw to Gavin Larsen.

Australia's second best batsman on the day was Steve Waugh but, coming in at number seven, he was invited to salvage the innings, not to shape it. Boon being a more conventional player, Australia's chances rested with Waugh's powerful forearms.

He struck gold once, putting Latham back over his head and into the sightscreen at the northern end for six, but with five overs remaining and the scoreboard showing an asking rate that had crept above ten per over — an event that was met with a chant of 'Kiwi, Kiwi' around the terraces — the odds were prohibitive.

The forty-sixth over of the Australian innings, bowled by Larsen, was the decisive one. Boon, by this time hobbling on his dicky right knee, brought up his century from the first ball, giving Steve Waugh the strike.

Larsen then deceived Waugh with a shorter ball, the bowler diving away to his right to complete a brilliant return catch as Waugh's attempt to force the pace miscued. If that blow had not shattered Australia's hopes, they were blown out of Auckland Harbour when Boon was run out two balls later, by a direct side-on hit by Chris Harris running in from deep mid-wicket.

It was a fittingly spectacular end to the boldest of cricketing coups.

Patrick Smith (editor) *The Age World Cup Cricket 1992* (1992)

Cricket tours are rich sources of incident. There have been several fine accounts of overseas trips by New Zealand teams, but my favourite is Don Cameron's *Caribbean Crusade*. Its excellence lies not so much in the match accounts, splendid though they are, for the 1971–72 series was not the most pulsating ever played and resulted in a 0–0 draw over five tests. What Cameron does so well is to conjure up the atmosphere, and paint a vivid picture of the kaleidoscope of territories in which the matches took place.

For the New Zealanders, St John's and Antigua will remain in the memory for a cricket match that would require A.G. Macdonnell, or perhaps Gilbert and Sullivan, to do it justice.

The cricket field, like the sun, rose in the east and set in the west and to the naked eye the drop seemed something like 10 to 15 feet. There were bumps and hollows, places of thick grass and others of bare soil laced with old bottle tops and pieces of glass. In the middle, in rather lonely level splendour, was the pitch which, like most of them in the West Indies, had been hammered into submission by hours of rolling. The men who did the rolling had time to spare, for they were the convicts from the gaol across the road and ground-staff duty was almost as welcome as parole.

Their uniform was a blue peaked cap, cream blouse and longish dark blue shorts — for all the world they looked like a bunch of overgrown schoolboys.

They were, their solitary and not too concerned guard told me, a fairly harmless lot. One had just missed a murder rap and was doing five years for manslaughter, but generally they were burglars, car converters and the like.

As ground staff they were champions. They could not do much about the undulations of the outfield or the sudden drop away to the western boundary, but when it came to removing or replacing the covers they were world-class. Without a command they would fasten to one edge of the cover and hurtle across the field, the cover billowing like some giant yellow butterfly behind them. Except once.

There was rain in the night before the second day's play, with Leewards Islands at the fag end of their first innings. The New Zealanders arrived a little more than an hour before the starting time of 11 a.m. The covers were still on, and on the covers were puddles. Dowling looked at Chapple, who looked at the book of words and then, without success, for the umpires who were in control of such matters as removing covers. No umpires.

Chapple looked at Dowling, Dowling looked at the puddles. Rocks were lifted, covers were slid away and, more by good luck than good management the pitch was affected only by two damp patches which looked dangerous but which served only to delay the start for an hour. The umpires had been summoned by an SOS call over the local radio station, and no-one seemed terribly upset that the covers had been removed, not strictly according to Hoyle. The prisoners, we later found, were not released until 10 a.m. that day, and so the covers had stayed.

So unfolded one of the more diverting games of cricket. Amid the fuss and bother over the covers, the drying-out of the patches and the late start, one of the umpires forgot the ball. On another occasion the bails went missing.

On the last day, when most of the sting had gone out of the game, Bob Cunis, promoted none too willingly to twelfth man, had to field. The game went on,

Cunis called for the ball, solemnly measured out his run, handed his hat to the umpire and made ready to bowl. He would have, too, had not the Leewards batsman realised what was happening and marched menacingly out of his crease.

On the last day, too, came the strange case of the early tea. The drinks had been taken out, an over bowled, and suddenly Bevan Congdon could be seen waving to his deep-set players to leave the field. Words were obviously being said in the middle. There was a flutter of interest in the pavilion. Had the Leewards declared, and left New Zealand a cakewalk to victory? Or had Congdon, as his agitated signals suggested, summoned his men from the field because of some dispute — thereby provoking another of the incidents to which the Leewards are not strangers?

Alas for hopes of victory for New Zealand, or sensational stories for the cricket presses of the world, the umpires had simply mistaken the time for tea, actually some 25 minutes distant. So there was time only for a brief laugh in the dressing room before the umpires and players marched out again.

Yet there was more to Antigua than this strange cricket match which, to be perfectly truthful, the New Zealanders did not play well.

There was, some miles to the south, a magnificent natural harbour which is known as Nelson's Dockyard, for Nelson spent much time there first as a junior officer and then as a captain in the King's Navy. Some of the original dockyard and buildings remain and if, like the elegant old cathedral in St John's, they are ever restored to their original state this harbour will rank as one of the wonders of the Caribbean.

The hinterland is not without beauty, either, and from any of the hills or small mountains you can see acres of rippling sugar-cane, with every now and then one of the old limestone crushing mills standing like sentry-boxes about the landscape.

Antiguans we met complained that they lived in a quiet backwater that the rest of the world passed by. Judging by what was going on in other parts of the world and, indeed, among their neighbours of the West Indies, perhaps being a quiet cosy backwater is not a bad idea.

D.J. Cameron *Caribbean Crusade* (1972)

Touring the Indian sub-continent is hard, so cricketing autobiographies say. There are the volatile crowds, the food, the heat, the need to take extra precautions against illness. But then, touring Australia seems to be equally difficult because the pitches, the opposing players and the partisan supporters, are as unyielding as toughened teak and rather less beautiful. And as for South Africa — you can just about be killed with kindness there. Spare a thought for those who have toured New Zealand. They sometimes found it tough going, too.

In 1876–77 James Lillywhite led a team of English professionals to Australasia. It was the second All-England team to visit this country, and the first to make a national tour. Since the business side of the enterprise was hopelessly mismanaged, the players had to find ways of augmenting the gate-takings in order to make a profit from their efforts. They appointed a couple of money-takers to sell souvenirs for them, put up their fleet-footed batsman, John Selby, to run races against all-comers for cash, and gambled on anything and everything — apart from the outcome of a match. The tour was a difficult one, full of incident, and marred by a betting scandal at the end, but no event was more extraordinary and dangerous than the journey recounted here.

At Greymouth the team met Mrs Radcliffe, the landlady of Warner's Commercial Hotel, Christchurch, and it was she, it would seem, who persuaded Lillywhite to travel overland by coach, across the southern mountains, rather than round the coast by steamer. Quite *why* the Englishmen agreed to entrust themselves to a hated Cobb's coach over 200 miles of mountain roads it is difficult to tell. Perhaps they had had enough of local steamers, drunken stewards and stuffy cabins. Perhaps the delightful Mrs Radcliffe had made them an offer they could not refuse. Whatever the cause, the luggage was sent on to Christchurch by sea, Ted Pooley being given the job of looking after it, whilst the rest of the team (plus their agent, two money-takers and a young Christchurch artist) prepared to take the scenic route with Mrs Radcliffe.

There was an inauspicious beginning. At the agreed starting time of 6.00 a.m. one player was missing, 'fancying some other person's bed better than his own' and a search of 'various places of resort' delayed them. Meanwhile Lillywhite and Bennett organized the party's distribution between the two coaches, (each to be pulled by four horses), rechecking the cricket bags which had been flung on the coaches' roofs.

It could not have been long before the players began to wonder if they had made the right decision to travel by land. As the coaches made their way up into the mountains, the cricketers frequently had to jump down and walk, mile after mile, ahead of the panting horses. When they climbed back on board for the descents, those on top would cling on grimly to avoid being shaken off (Collins the money-taker providing a terrible warning, when he dozed off, fell into the road, and narrowly avoided being run over), whilst those sitting inside on the benches would hit their heads on the roof every time a wheel jumped over a pothole. The road, when not climbing up or running down a mountain, followed the courses of rivers, which frequently had to be crossed, sometimes by ferry, sometimes by ford. Flooded rivers, like the Taipo, half-a-mile across, presented a very real hazard: 'It is no easy matter', wrote Southerton, 'for a coachman to drive over such a track, the water rearing over the boulders as large as coach wheels, now up, now down, with a thump enough to break them into splinters, and sending the inside passengers from one side to the other.' To increase their discomfort, by mid-afternoon it was pouring with rain and by nightfall Lillywhite and Ulyett, sitting on the box seats, were soaked through.

Eighteen hours into the journey, at midnight, as the rain continued to pour down, they reached the famous Otira River and Gorge. Southerton and his fellows in the first coach were told to cross the swollen river on foot, by means of a narrow wooden bridge, which proved inadequate. One player fell through and was, with difficulty, rescued; the rest, finding the bridge broken off, were forced to wade through the rising river: 'There we were in the bed of the river, with the elements as bad as anyone can possibly imagine; on either side of us were mountains 3000 feet high, the river rising rapidly, no one knowing which way to move in the utter darkness, and not a soul to hear us, shout as loud as we could...' At this critical moment the lights of the coach, coming through the waters, appeared from the darkness and Southerton's party, drenched to the skin, swam, rode or waded with it. Safe on the far side, they stumbled over boulders and stumps of trees towards a stone cottage, called the Otira Hotel, where they divested themselves of their wet clothes and leapt into the four small beds which, said Southerton, were all the hotel had to offer.

The second coach, containing Mrs Radcliffe, Lillywhite and six others, was less lucky. They had tried to drive through but a horse fell down and they found themselves stranded in the middle of the swollen river, which was rapidly rising. The coachman shouted to the players to alight and help him raise the horse. At first, in fear, they refused, but when he screamed that they were in danger of drowning, they jumped out in a hurry, Charlwood catching his foot in his ulster coat and falling in head first. Eventually they raised the horse and, amidst an ever rising torrent, the stranded coach was pulled, boulder by boulder, to safety. Ulyett reckoned that he swam most of the way across, but Armitage, carrying Mrs Radcliffe on his shoulders, must have found an easier fording place.

Inside the hotel at last, they demanded drink, consumed the sum total of the premises (three bottles of very rough brandy) and stripped off their wet clothes. Standing in bare feet on the swimming stone floor, they wrung their clothes in front of the fire which the first coach party had lit. They had nothing else to wear for their main luggage was somewhere on the seas with Pooley, whilst their cricket bags were wet through. With admirable stoicism they filled their pipes and smoked their way through what remained of the night. There were no chairs, but a few tried sleeping on tables, or even on the floor wrapped in blankets…

The next morning dawned bright and fine so the All-England Eleven put out their overcoats and shoes to dry. There being nothing to eat, the owner of the house set off with his horse and gun and returned in about two hours with a sheep, which the players helped cut up and roast. Ulyett meanwhile made some bread cakes, tending them with the only implement available, a hayfork. By noon it was raining again but the coaches set out once more in the early afternoon. However, two miles up the road they came across a landslide and were forced to return to spend a second night at Otira. Once more it was a question of making the best of a difficult time, smoking their pipes and playing cards deep into the night, for the floors and tables offered little chance of sleep.

The reminiscences of both Southerton and Ulyett fail to mention how Mrs Radcliffe, the Christchurch landlady, spent these nights. However, Alf Shaw, who usually followed Southerton's account slavishly for his own book of reminiscences, for once put in details entirely of his own: 'The lady passenger, whom Armitage so gallantly carried through the flood, was made as comfortable for the night as circumstances would permit by the woman who was in charge of the shanty'. It is possible, however, that this prim chaperoning is simply a gloss, pandering to the sensibilities of the readers of 1902. Moreover, the accounts vary mysteriously about the number of available beds, Ulyett recalling that five jumped into the only one. There, perhaps, one should hastily abandon conjecture of Mrs Radcliffe's whereabouts at Otira.

At a quarter to five the next morning the journey recommenced in pouring rain and it ended 18 hours later on the plains of Canterbury. This was a further gruelling time, involving more ascents and descents of narrow, precipitous tracks (Charlwood so nervous that he took to running behind his coach), more hard walking (once across a plank with 100-foot drops below) and more river crossings, at one of which Tom Emmett and Harry Jupp came to blows. Jupp, riding inside the coach and comparatively dry, had taken exception to being asked to get out and wade across a deep river, whilst Emmett, who was already soaked to the skin, continued to sit on the box. Accordingly, Jupp climbed up and pulled Tom Emmett off his seat.

By late evening on the third day of their trek they reached Porter's Pass, with a startling view of a valley 6000 feet below; one final descent brought them to Sheffield, the end of their 60-hour coach journey. But even here their saga of misadventure continued, for there was no train ready to take them on to Christchurch, and they had to spend one further uncomfortable night, smoking their pipes or sleeping on a hotel's sofas and floor. One can imagine their mixed emotions next day at 9.30 a.m. as they were met at Christchurch station by the sportsmen of Canterbury and driven in state in a drag to Warner's Commercial Hotel, run by Mrs Radcliffe's husband. There they had a quick bath, a big breakfast, read letters from home (forwarded from Melbourne by Conway), and then returned to the drag to go out to play against the Christchurch Eighteen†.

Anthony Meredith *Summers in Winter* (1990)

† In the early years of New Zealand cricket, it was usual for overseas teams to play against more than 11 opponents.

Time was when tours were leisurely affairs. Because visiting teams were less frequent, their arrival was often a great social event. Sometimes tourists were even billeted with local people. The England Women's team that toured Australia and New Zealand in 1948–49 was a strong side, led by the great Molly Hide and blessed with a number of free-scoring players, including all-rounder Myrtle MacLagan and the big-hitting Mary 'Johnnie' Johnson. This extract comes from a diary kept by one of the team and seems to breathe the true spirit of cricket: a game through which friendships can be forged, a game to be shared — above all, a game to be enjoyed.

We wake up in the pink sheets, and amid the trim furnishings, of Elsie and Murray Vernon's bright new home on the outskirts of Greymouth. Murray is an upholsterer and a keen cricketer: Elsie, whom he met in London, a true cockney with a non-stop flow of chatter.

After a mayoral reception attended by representatives from all the West Coast sporting organizations, we drive up the Arnold Valley to the Ngahere Gold Dredge, and from there to the mining village of Blackball, to be accorded a most royal reception by Mr and Mrs Hugh Dowling, and practically the entire population of Blackball. For we find ourselves immediately surrounded by friendly miners and diggers, some with beards, some with towels round their necks, all work-stained and weary, for they have come in to see us straight off the shift. Soon we are all chattering away merrily — photos are taken — enormous conviviality develops. For pure spontaneity our Blackball welcome among the miners just about beats the band.

Match v. West Coast at Greymouth, Saturday, March 5, 1949

There is a local joke that it always rains in Greymouth. But not on us: as we walk down to the Recreation Ground, matting-wicketed, the crisp morning air is soon warmed by a hot sun.

Myrtle puts the West Coast in to bat, which they do with more stubbornness than conviction, for although their total is but 44, it takes us until lunchtime to remove them.

At the opening of our innings, West Coast's hopes run high, for Netta, indulging too soon her penchant for a playful cow-shot, presents them with an easy wicket. But Robbie, Mary D. and Megan do much as they like with the bowling, Megan, a very much improved bat these days, being the fastest scorer of the three of them.

While all this is going on Molly and I chat with an old cricketer, a Mr O'Donnell, who bowled Sir Pelham Warner first ball in the year 1903, and has kept up a desultory correspondence with him ever since. It has certainly been very desultory of recent years, for in 1940 Sir Pelham sent Mr O'Donnell a line of greeting via a mutual acquaintance in His Majesty's Forces. This military gentleman, however, lost his kitbag for the period of the war, with the result that Mr O'Donnell has only just received the letter. Seven years in the post, you might say. We promise that, when next we see Sir Pelham, we will convey to him Mr O'Donnell's acknowledgement and salutations.

Greymouth gives us a warmhearted and enjoyable farewell dinner at the Albion Hotel, and next morning, sped on our way by our friends the Vernons, we set off for Christchurch through the Lewis Pass.

Another lovely drive, and then, after lunch at the Mariwa Springs Hotel, we drive on several hours, until the mountains give place to open rolling country. And we think of tea. A cup of tea would be just the thing. But we reckon without the New Zealand Sunday, a forlorn institution for the traveller if ever there was one. We try three hotels, but they have no staff, and they don't care a fig whether we have a cup of tea or no. If the government intend to attract foreign visitors to the country, something drastic will have to be done to the hotel proprietors. So far as we can judge, the New Zealand scenery is without parallel, and her sporting facilities unique, but neither will attract tourists in the absence of good hotel accommodation.

We arrive in Christchurch very late.

Match v. Canterbury at Christchurch, Tuesday, March 8 and Wednesday, March 9, 1949

Canterbury are eventually beaten, but by no means disgraced, and the newspaper corespondents are quick to notice that in fielding the home side suffers not at all in comparison with ourselves.

Hagley Park provides a thoroughly English setting, and the chilly nip which has succeeded Monday's rain reminds us of cricketing conditions at home. Molly, winning the toss, decides to give Canterbury the worst of a wicket which is bound to be queer, to say the least of it. And Canterbury do not find it easy. Phil Blackler, already chosen for the New Zealand test team and the possessor of an astronomical batting average in local club games, comes up to expectations as the side's best batsman, her short innings including four fours. The later batsmen also stage something of a recovery, the last two wickets yielding 30 runs to bring the total to 99.

England's innings, with a total of 177, does not go according to plan. To be sure Myrtle gets her 50 in reasonable time, but Robbie's 28 in 80 minutes might well have been quicker. Molly, whom the crowd all hope to see, is run out at 13 by an excellent return from Blackler at cover, Wilkie is caught at square leg, Hazel is caught, Barbara is bowled, and I make things no better by promptly running out Johnnie. But Mary D. is in great form, driving beautifully straight past the bowler. When she gains greater confidence Mary will do very well, for it is a treat to see her use her strength to hit the ball so hard. It is also worth recording that in this innings the Canterbury wicket-keeper does not allow a single bye.

Batting again next morning, the home side can achieve only 69, leaving us winners by an innings and nine runs.

The following day, Frank and Yvonne Bridger, with whom we have been so happily billeted, see us on to the train for Dunedin.

In Dunedin I am borne off by Dr Elizabeth Gregory, Dean of the Faculty of Home Science at Otago's famous university, who drives me straight up a hill like the side of a house to a little home with the most magnificent view over the harbour one could ever hope to see. I watch this scene for some time, being unable to trap my hostess, who is darting round the house like a streak of lightning making dispositions for my comfort. When at last she can be persuaded to anchor and be inspected at close quarters, I discover that learning is here allied to a pair of blue eyes and a merry sense of humour, and that a life dedicated to biochemistry can still include people and tennis and fun.

Match v. Otago at Dunedin, Saturday, March 12, 1949

Chilly weather for cricket. For my job as scorer I attire myself in shirt, skirt, jersey, jacket, top coat and rug and then am none too warm.

Otago, put in to bat in the damp morning, compile 88 runs. They have some very promising young players, who have been coached to move their feet and go after the ball, and Mrs Blackie, their captain, who has been chosen for the New Zealand team, shows the makings of a good bat before she is bowled by Maclagan. And we are interested to find that Miss Sew Hoy, who bats second wicket down, is Chinese by nationality, her family having lived in Dunedin for many years. She defends stubbornly for half an hour, and makes two runs. Their seventh wicket partnership, however, between a 15-year-old schoolgirl called Butler, and Mrs Morris, their best bowler, proves most fruitful. We are much impressed by the way these two pick out a loose ball: this is the best batting we have seen in New Zealand.

But the bowling is not up to the same standard, and the scorer has a hair-raising afternoon of it in her endeavours to record the scoring of 424 runs in the right places. Mrs Morris does well to take five wickets for 84, for to the evident satisfaction of the large crowd, today we seem bent on murder — Myrtle 112, Robbie 67, Molly 62, Hazel 46, Mary D. 30. At the end of the day Johnnie, well primed, is on the hunt for sixes. Her first one misses a car windscreen by a hair's breadth, but her second has the misfortune to lay out a lady who is walking along the public footpath of the road that skirts the ground. This is more than poor Johnnie bargained for. The St John Ambulance people are summoned immediately, and we are all much relieved to hear that the blow, which might have been serious, proved only a superficial one.

Otago again make about 70 in their second innings, and again Mrs Morris is their top scorer, though Mrs Blackie plays some pretty shots.

Another sad departure next morning, for we must travel back to Christchurch to board the ferry for Wellington. Dr Gregory has been a most kind hostess, and I have enjoyed a glimpse of university life.

Nancy Joy **Maiden Over** (1950)

If ever a match could be described as inspirational, it was the second test between New Zealand and South Africa on the 1953–54 tour. It had no fairy-tale ending, but it included one of the bravest day's cricket ever played. Of the many accounts that have been written about the event, this, to me, is the most immediate and moving. After reading it, who would dare describe cricket as a boring game in which nothing ever happens?

The second day of the second test [26 December 1953] dawned trag-ically. At 5 a.m. Bob Blair learned of the death of his fiancée in the fearful rail disaster at Tangiwai.

In this incredible accident, waters from the crater lake of Mount Ruapehu escaped underground and flooded down the mountainside, smashing the rail bridge at Tangiwai minutes before a holiday express came thundering through the night; 151 people died in this Christmas tragedy.

Twenty-three thousand spectators basked in the sun at Ellis Park and could not know of the heavy sadness in the hearts of the New Zealand cricketers who arrived at the ground. Bob Blair stayed at the hotel.

This was the notorious green wicket at Ellis Park — the most dangerous wicket I have played on, and especially with a genuine fast bowler like Neil Adcock operating. I remember inspecting the wicket with Geoff Rabone and he commenting to the groundsman about the long grass on the wicket. In places the blades were 3 inches long and merely rolled flat. This, accord-ing to the groundsman, would have a 'cushioning effect on the ball'! The only cushioning the ball got that day was when it pounded into ribs, chest and head.

On the first day it played tolerably well, but we tossed our chances to the winds by putting down seven catches. At the end of the day South Africa was 259 for 8. There was no play Christmas Day and on Boxing Day the flags of the Union and the Dominion hung pathetically at half-mast over the stand, marking the personal and national loss at Tangiwai.

We quickly picked up the last two South African wickets that morning and then the fun, such as it was, started. We lost two quick wickets with Adcock rampant from the first ball. Then Sutcliffe tried desperately to hook a flyer, missed and took a terrible blow on the left ear. He collapsed and for the first time in cricket I saw a stretcher rushed to the pitch. Bert struggled to his feet, and assured me groggily he was O.K. as I walked in to replace him. I had my doubts, for as I took guard I was standing in a patch of blood.

It was with a quite unrealistic feeling of determination and nervousness that I patted my bat and saw Adcock loping in. The first ball slammed into my side. Determination for the first time dominated nervousness. The second ball flashed through to the same tender spot — and so did three more in that first, dangerous over.

Adcock was pitching just short of a length outside my off stick and seaming back and lifting viciously off the grass 'cushion'. This was fast bowling as I had never seen it before and my technique was lacking. It was not long before, and perhaps, inevitable that my edge saw Russell Endean take a magnificent diving catch off Adcock.

Laurie Miller passed me on the way to the wickets with a wry quirk of the eyebrow and was immediately hit heavily on the chest playing forward to a rising ball. He was obviously in considerable pain and coughing blood, but faced another ball, took a single off the hip and then was persuaded to leave the field.

Into this atmosphere came a boy. John Beck, only 19, walked in to play his first test innings and, with youth's resilience, he played his strokes. He saw Matt Poore bowled off his body by Adcock and replaced by Frank Mooney. Young John was out after an hour for 16 and Miller, against doctor's advice, came out again. He hit 14 in a hurry and Mooney struck determinedly.

In the meantime, Sutcliffe had collapsed again during X-ray examinations, but with his head swathed in bandages he walked through the tunnel on to the ground as Miller walked back. The acclaim pounded at our ears. This was a Sutcliffe with slaughter in his mind. He hit an Ironside in-swinger over long-on for six and that set the character of an innings of classic quality. Cheetham brought Adcock back and Sutcliffe sought retribution immediately by square-cutting him viciously to the fence. He hit Tayfield mercilessly for a straight six and the follow-on was saved. He lost Mooney after an invaluable defensive hand; MacGibbon and Overton came and went and with the board showing 154 for 9 that was that. There was no possibility of Blair batting and the players moved toward the tunnel.

No possibility.... Unknown to us watching this dramatic display, Bob Blair had arrived from the hotel after hearing of our plight. There was a giant's sigh from the crowd as he moved slowly through the mouth of the tunnel. Sutcliffe walked to meet him, put his arm around his shoulders and walked with him to the wicket.

The crowd stood as one. In silence.

This was the most unforgettable moment of my life. Tears streamed unchecked down the cheeks of those around me, and down my own. To be hurt physically and return to fight I can understand. To be so deeply bruised mentally and emotionally and return, took a kind of courage which passed understanding.

Sutcliffe was inspired. He thrashed Tayfield for 19 in an over — three huge sixes and a single to retain the strike. The crowd's noise surged deafeningly. There was one ball left in the over. Blair bent over his bat. We waited with a sort of fearful hope. Bob watched Tayfield move in, then swung him magnificently into the tumultuous, hysterically cheering crowd. Soon afterwards he was stumped.

New Zealand's failure in the second innings, South Africa's victory — these were mere appendages to the drama. December 26 took the glory.

J.R. Reid *Sword of Willow* (1962)

FOUR

MORE THAN THE PLAYERS

Players are the main focus of any match, yet they are only part of the complete cricketing experience. Before a game can take place there needs to be a ground to play it on. New Zealand has some fascinating grounds, from the classic oval of the Basin Reserve — such a superb venue if Wellington's notorious winds are in a kindly mood — to the eccentric Valley of Peace, home of the Christchurch Cinema's Cricket Club, which is out-of-bounds to half the population because women are forbidden to set foot there.

One ground in New Zealand is so striking and unusual that some well travelled observers have nominated it as the most beautiful in the world.

Pukekura Park, New Plymouth, is unique. The ground is cut out of a hill, so that the slopes on three sides of the ground would rise sheer from the playing area if they had not been terraced and the terraces then turfed (which would not require a tremendous effort because on this wonderful volcanic soil it only needs a handful of grass seed to be tossed onto the ground and almost overnight you have a lawn). The spectators take deck chairs and loungers on to the terraces, place them around tables and enjoy their cricket in, literally, a picnic atmosphere. The whole area is made up of botanical gardens and a lake (filled by small streams which filter down through the woods). And at the eastern end of the lake the snow-capped peak of Mount Egmont presides benignly over the scene. It is utterly breathtaking. The only open side of the ground looks out over the blue — oh, *so* blue — waters of the Tasman and really this is no place to play any sort of fiercely competitive cricket. It should be used as an antipodean Glyndebourne to stage Mozart.

Don Mosey *The Best Job in the World* (1985)

Given time, cricket grounds develop their own mystique. When R.T. Brittenden set out to describe the first match ever played for the Plunket Shield, the fore-runner of today's Shell Trophy, he found himself trying to capture, as well, the spirit and history of the ground on which the game took place.

October in Christchurch is a fascinating month, marked by a dozen local traditions. Employees of the City Council put out in their punts to clean the weeds from the bed of the Avon, nurses from the public hospital have their photographs taken among the daffodil glades, neighbours exchange branches of their blossom trees, the willows along the river bank begin to assume the graceful poses which will be recorded on the calendars posted at Christmas.

In a score of parks, batsmen inspect the first of the season's slow long hops with grave suspicion, bowlers recover their lbw voices, and find they withstand the years better than arms or legs or wind; untidy scorers demand of absent-minded player-umpires whether 'that was a hit or a bye', and captains, the happiest and most harassed of all cricketers, begin their summer vocation of making silk purses from sows' ears, while exercising the restraint and tact of successful diplomats — if there are such creatures.

The centre of all this cricketing activity in Christchurch is the oval at Hagley Park, described by a good many visitors to New Zealand as the loveliest ground in the world. Beauty cannot be measured mathematically, and comparisons between Hagley and other cricket grounds are as useless as they are inconclusive.

Test and Plunket Shield matches are played at Lancaster Park; but cricket's heart beats at Hagley. At Lancaster Park there is the hard light of publicity on the player's every action. The view seems to be restricted to the scoreboard and the gasometer. At a big match, the dust swirling off the embankment settles on the paper bags and beer bottles. At Hagley, a corpulent second slip may have the ball cut squarely on to his shin without having to parade his indignity before derisive thousands. There are no turnstiles, and although the cricket is good — horseplay at Hagley would be almost irreligious — it has a friendliness and a happiness born, one must suppose, of the serenity of the surroundings and the companionship of cricket. Lancaster Park is as much a cricket ground as Hagley; but it is a cricket of Sheffield or Leeds. Hagley might have been lifted from the heart of Kent.

The first overseas cricket team to play in Christchurch was Parr's All-England Eleven, in February, 1864. Canterbury had then been founded only 13 years, and the touring team was astounded to find a good ground, fenced, and with a new pavilion typical of English cricket architecture of the time.

In September, 1864, the Canterbury Provincial Council granted the Christchurch Cricket Club the lease of 30 acres of Hagley Park, nearer the city than the prepared ground, and construction of the new ground began almost immediately. The council wisely stipulated that the public must always have the right of access to the area, and it was thus saved from becoming an arena.

A man called Souter put down the first pitch at the new ground, and he brought down the original turf, in dray loads. It was relaid, piece by piece, and English grasses sown. Souter, an extraordinarily skilful man at putting down and caring for lawns, had an aversion to mowers, especially where grass had not been long established, and for a considerable period nothing but a scythe was used on the grass — but those who recalled the ground in its early years said it was scythed so well that it looked machine-cut. The pavilion from the original ground was also brought down, long lines of trees were planted, live fences established, wells sunk, and the first club match was played in November, 1866.

The pavilion is still there, nearly 100 years of age, and it is still used throughout the summer months. From it some of the world's greatest cricketers — among them Spofforth, Boyle, Ulyett, Shaw, Lillywhite, Bannerman — have gone out to play. On this ground, Canterbury made the first score of more than 300 in inter-provincial cricket; in 1881 G. Watson scored the first representative century by a New Zealander, for Canterbury against Otago at Hagley; eight years later A.E. Moss, whose personal story was one of tragedy and subsequent triumph, became the only bowler in the world to take all ten wickets in an innings in his first-class debut — and he did it at Hagley.

So Hagley matured, and the legends were born beneath the sturdy elms and oaks. But it had one more contribution to make to the history of New Zealand cricket before being left to club and minor representative games. It was there, in 1907, that the first Plunket Shield match was played.

When the shield was presented by Lord Plunket, a Governor-General of New Zealand, the New Zealand Cricket Council decided that on the basis of the previous season's performances Canterbury should be the first holder. The decision was not well received; then, as now, the council had its critics. The first to challenge — the present competitive system, with each team meeting all the others, did not begin until 1921–22 — was Auckland. So started a series of matches which has been the backbone of New Zealand cricket.

The matches begin each year at Christmas, and are as much a part of the Christmas tradition as roast lamb and green peas. Occasionally, it must be admitted, the cricket has done little more than persuade the spectator to yield to the after-dinner languor of the occasion, but if the standards have not always been high, the shield competition has offered wonderful entertainment, many hours and days of excitement.

Of the cricket in the first Plunket Shield match, not very much can be said, for Auckland was far too strong, and the game was not particularly interesting, competitively. But it was a great occasion, graced by some of the greatest of New Zealand players.

Canterbury had Dan Reese, regarded as one of the greatest of New Zealand all-rounders. His dynamic driving is still recalled fondly. He played county cricket in England for a period and in New Zealand scored nearly 3000 runs, and took more than 100 wickets. Billy Patrick, a stylist with a fatal lack of restraint, had a long and successful career; Hugh Lusk was a schoolmaster who taught New Zealand the value of the pull stroke; Joe Bennett was the essence of accuracy with his medium-paced bowling, and Boxshall was one of the characters of Canterbury cricket. He had a library in Cathedral Square, which helped make him a familiar figure. Short and rotund, he wore an ample white moustache, but as a wicketkeeper he was incredibly quick, so quick that there were some who said he could not do what he did and do it legally. A left-hander and a willing hitter, he was always given a tremendous reception when he came out to bat.

The Auckland stars were Brook-Smith, a player who had a long career for his province; Hemus, a lightly built but graceful and accomplished batsman with a magnificent defence and Relf, the Sussex professional. Tall and dark, Relf had all the shots, and at Hagley he showed Canterbury the lot.

He was a most talented cricketer, and had been invited to play with the English team in Australia, but had been unable to accept because of his engagement with the Auckland association.

The preparations for the match were elaborate, although there was a suggestion of the casual in the meeting of the Canterbury team a few days before the game, when 'Reese was elected captain'. The public interest in the match, fanned by the claims that Canterbury should not have been awarded the shield, was such that the burning down of Parliament Buildings in Wellington — described in one newspaper as a 'magnificent sight' — claimed only passing notice. Wool was still fetching from 2½d. to 1s. 3d. a pound, and there was a cricket match to consider.

This was one of the few occasions on which scoring cards were printed for the benefit of spectators, with the players' numbers on the board, English fashion. The pitch was hard and true, and the ground, after mid-week showers, was a picture. The money taken at the gate was £81, a trifling sum today, but two years earlier, a three-day game at Lancaster Park against the Australians had brought in only £55 16s. 3d.

Canterbury began most confidently, with Lusk and Patrick. Lusk showed rare judgement with his cutting and pulling, and Patrick played soundly, although worried by the left-hand spinner Kerr. They shared an opening partnership of 93, yet the side was all out for 190. Relf's easy, swinging delivery, his length and accuracy and stamina were too much for batsmen who seemed to feel that all the bowlers should be thrashed all the time.

Relf bowled the first over in Plunket Shield cricket, a maiden to Lusk, but the 50 was up in 40 minutes, and Lusk reached his half-century in an hour. He was out to the first ball after lunch, caught at the wicket. Reese played a reckless but entertaining innings. He drove successive balls from Howden for four, four, six, and hit another six before he was out. Boxshall hit three fours in an over from Relf, but Canterbury was all out by 4 p.m., largely, it seemed, because of its superiority complex.

Auckland started just as briskly, the 100 being reached in an hour and a quarter, whereupon Brook-Smith was caught behind off the leg-spin bowler Malone. Anthony made a magnificent slip catch to dismiss Mason, but at the close of play Auckland was 170 for two, with Hemus a polished 63 not out.

The second day was another of brilliant sunshine, and Canterbury began well by having Cummings caught at the wicket before a run had been added. But that was the last success for a considerable period. Although Bennett rarely bowled better, he could do not more than keep the scoring rate within reasonable limits, while at the other end the good bowling was hit as hard and often as the bad.

Hemus continued to play delightfully, while Relf, beautifully correct, stylish, forceful and completely nonchalant, cut, drove and pulled his way through the morning. By lunch, Auckland was 312 for 3, and there was little consolation for Canterbury in the knowledge that both batsmen had been dropped behind off Bennett.

They went on to 347 — a partnership of 177 — before Boxshall caught Hemus, and still Relf laid about him. In Haddon he had an aggressive partner, and the 400 was reached in five hours. The later batsmen threw their bats at everything, and Canterbury was in again soon after 5 p.m. with a deficit of 349. At the end of the afternoon 88 had been scored, for two wickets, at express speed, Reese having hit seven fours and a six in his 42.

On a lovely last day, the main contributions came from the fast but erratic bowling of Haddon, and the violence of Orchard, the only man who has hit a ball over the pavilion at Lancaster Park. A great athlete and rugby player, he hooked and drove with tremendous power in making his 51, but Canterbury was clearly conscious of defeat all the way, and the game ended in mid-afternoon.

Since that December day 50 years ago, another 250 Plunket Shield matches have been played. But the succession started at Hagley; thousands of cricketers, from the test match great to the third change bowlers in fourth grade teams, have walked the same firm turf for more than 90 years, and have learned to love it. At day's end the stumps cast long shadows across the soft grass to the mellowing timbers of the ancient pavilion. At this green pool of peace, cricket history has been written, and with it some pretty stories. Perhaps it was a necessary part of growing up that Plunket Shield matches should leave these idyllic surrounds behind, but it was a pity.

R.T. Brittenden *Great Days in New Zealand Cricket* (1958)

If cricket grounds contribute greatly to the atmosphere of a match, so do those much-maligned and frequently undervalued characters, the umpires.

There we were, my cousin Jack from Texas and I, sitting in the late summer sun on the terraces at Eden Park watching a one-dayer between New Zealand and England. Jack was having trouble keeping his mind on the game; he knew the Dallas Cowboys but he didn't have a clue about cricket. He spent most of his time checking out other people sitting around us. But at one point Jack stared out at the wicket where Richard Hadlee and Jeff Crowe had formed a desperate batting partnership hoping to salvage a tie.

'Tell me,' said Jack, 'why do they have doctors out there?'

'What?'

'Those doctors, in the white coats.'

I explained, but as far as Jack was concerned whether they were doctors or umpires was academic. He nodded perfunctorily and began looking in other directions again probably wondering when he'd finally get to see the glow worms.

For my part I kept my eye on the umpires for a moment; giving them attention they normally don't receive. After all, who pays to watch an umpire? They are as much a part of the game as players, but unless a decision is needed on an lbw or a run out, who cares? But that is precisely why I watched them, for a change.

I wondered. Why would anyone in their right mind want to be a cricket umpire? It doesn't look like a lot of fun standing out there in the hot sun all day. They don't bat or chase after the ball. They suffer sore feet, backache, without exception they must pay strict attention to every ball played, and they have to listen for inaudible ticks of the ball off the bat above all other sounds while trying to establish a policy on lbws.

A cricket umpire might have won Lotto the night before or fallen in love or lost his best friend, but when he steps out onto the pitch to umpire he's not supposed to show any emotion at all. What's more, cricket umpires are often not even paid! They *volunteer* to suffer restraint. And if they are paid they get so little one could never justify doing it for the money.

It seems to be just as English umpire David Constant described it in his book on the subject, 'a thankless task. Few people come up to you and say "well umpired".'

Tom Hyde 'Men in White Coats', **Metro** February 1989

To most cricket lovers, there is another indispensable part of the summer game. Even if we cannot be there, we are still able to soak up the atmosphere and experience the highs and lows of a match through the magic of radio. Hard as television tries, it has not yet replaced the friendly sound of the radio commentary that filters into homes and work places as people go about their daily lives.

In our house it's called the 'horrible voice'. It starts in November, breaks briefly for Christmas and is still going well into March. It is the ritual accompaniment to all the lawn-mowing, fence-mending and attempted bronzing. It is 1000 variations on a single magic patter; the rhythm of the Kiwi summer. A thousand variations on: 'Morrison runs in to bowl...and Gooch pushes quietly into the covers.' Horrible voice? To me it's music.

Years ago, before I had learnt of the horrible voice, the efforts of Turner and Collinge would come crackling out of a shortwave hidden under my pillow — encounters made illicit by the exotic and distant sound of the commentary; men who talked into bowls of water and discussed mysterious faraway places — the Vauxhall end, the Nursery end, the Lord's ridge.

It was radio then, and it is radio now, through which I see cricket. A game played on fields and pitches invented in the imagination, commented upon by men who exist only as comforting voices.

How would I like to spend a day with the commentators? A dream come true. But also a dream that might have to end there — might end as the characters of my imagination are replaced by human, and perhaps flawed, in-the-flesh incarnations.

Saturday, 9.50 a.m., Lancaster Park. New Zealand have won the toss and put England in to bat. Inside the Radio New Zealand commentary box there isn't quite enough room for the eight Metalon chairs onto which climb three commentators, three comments people, a scorer, a technician and one journalist. It always sounded bigger on radio. And that's before Jeremy Coney's legs arrived.

Peter Sharp puts up the first session's roster. He has lost the toss and is first in. Half an hour at a time for Sharp, Bryan Waddle and Iain Gallaway, today's commentators; an hour each for Coney and Chris O'Malley, the comments people.

Waddle enters the box. He's the senior commentator, the boss — in as much as someone has to be the boss. His arrival sparks off a stream of light-hearted banter. Who's going to do Richard Hadlee's 'Knight Report' for TV since Hadlee is off sick? Someone suggests they could do it as the 'Peasant's Report'. Coney comes in, paisley *One World of Sport* tie and all. 'Now we know what you had for dinner,' taunts Waddle. You sense that these guys are doing what they most want to do.

England 46 for 3. Gower, Atherton and Gooch out cheaply. Coney points me in the direction of Peter Sharp's right foot. It's twitching and trembling with every Willie Watson delivery. Commentators twitch. This business, it seems, taxes the body as well as the soul.

When Coney is at the mike he leans towards Waddle, accenting his points with a florid wave of his long left arm. They're the pair at the bar, arguing, bantering and talking as the fifth jug slips by. Waddle in turn scans the horizon through binoculars, diligent to any quiet change in the field. He has been had before. In the West Indies Martin and Jeff Crowe swapped their traditional positions just to catch him out.

According to Waddle, commentating is exhausting work. 'At the end of the day you're absolutely stuffed. There is a lot of energy up there.' Coney agrees. 'You should weigh us as we go in and as we go out.' And that's not counting work done in places like India and Pakistan.

Each of the team has their favourite horror story. Gallaway's is the time he had to commentate from up a tree in Pakistan; Waddle talks with horror of doing a five-day test in India all on his own, suffering from a case of the trots but unable to leave the commentary box (Coney was back at the hotel, also sick). Coney's tale remembers well the Indian headphones — evidently not built with his larger New Zealand head in mind.

Coney believes in radio — he says it is the perfect medium through which to view cricket. 'The view is 365 degrees. You can see anything that's going on within the mind's eye... With television you talk through a very small window and it's a very selective window. It doesn't offer the whole picture at all. And the bigger side has always been important to me.'

Radio also gives people like Coney, an English and drama teacher by background, or Gallaway, a self-confessed fan of language, the chance to let loose with their vocabularies. As Waddle points out, there are only so many types of cricket shot. So, up in the box, you hear the latest descriptions being tested. There's 'nurdling' (as in 'Crowe nurdles the ball down to fine-leg'), a term invented to describe a gently caressed leg-glance. Peter Sharp comes up with the 'swook', a shot somewhere between a sweep and a hook, and a 'swish', which is mostly like a miss.

England 230 for 7 after 50 overs. I use the lunch break to pick Waddle's brain. What about those Aussie commentators, the Max Walkers and Tony Greigs of this world, who tormented us through January with their own brand of cricketing jingo-babble?

Waddle: 'I can't believe that those guys who played cricket can bad-mouth guys currently playing the game. When you hear Geoff Boycott talk about the slowness of some player you've got to ask yourself, "Did he score a 100 every time he went out to bat and do it at better than a run a ball?"

'It's unfair on the players, it's unfair on the public. They treat the public as idiots, and the minute you start doing that you're on a hiding to nothing — none of them are idiots.'

New Zealand has reached 210 for 5, with Rutherford and Harris doing the recovery job, and tension in the box is rising. Pieces of green paper, the scorer's system for communicating with the commentators, are starting to fly; the minutes for Rutherford's 50, Harris's top score for New Zealand.

The cellphone rings, the producer's sole method of talking to his wards. Unfortunately, no one knows how to answer it and the shrill bleeping continues until the technically literate Waddle can complete his dash.

Bicknell bowls a would-be wide but the umpire remains unmoved. Sharp's arms shoot out in an exaggerated and frustrated wide gesture. Yes, they're just the littlest bit parochial. As Waddle puts it, 'People don't want to hear you doing a downer on your own people.'

Half an hour later and Rutherford and Harris are out. Gavin Larsen comes in to an impossible situation, swooks away at De Freitas but to no avail. England have won by 14 runs. Sharp and Waddle further loosen their already loose ties. They're trying to be positive. It's the team's golden rule — be positive. It's what cricket is all about for them.

'Cricket commentators are people who look at the hills over there and see a rainbow,' says Coney. 'They see things in a different way. And with cricket there is always a funny side — it's like life itself.

'People say cricket is deadly dull, but to me it's never dull. There can be so much happen in one delivery that you can never describe it all.

'Just as long as you always think of your listener. We are in their ear. We are literally in their ear. You're listening to the cricket as you paint the house and we might be having a discussion or an argument. You can be taken into the action. You're involved. I think it is a lovely process to go through.'

Listening to Coney, looking back at the box, I allow myself one final indulgence. It's taken years, but at last I think I know what I want to be when I grow up.

Paul Huggett 'In the Box Seat' *New Zealand Listener* 11 March 1991

Commentating in New Zealand is not necessarily an easy job, as a distinguished visitor from England's *Test Match Special* programme once discovered.

My first day's commentary in New Zealand did not start well. In England we do not mount commentary of every game a touring side plays but in New Zealand they do, and I had been asked to join their commentary team for every match. As I was not doing any commentaries back to England — simply reports and features — I was very happy to do so because if there is anything better in life than watching cricket it is watching it and talking about it at the same time. Many followers of the game like to go alone and simply watch in appreciative silence; others prefer the shared pleasure of watching and discussing it with a companion. Of the two schools of thought I much prefer the latter, and better even than that is the privilege — for it is a very great privilege — of describing what I see to an audience of those who cannot see it. Or to most of whom cannot see it…

Just to the left of the commentary box at Eden Park, Auckland, and a little in front, is an area called Cans Corner. There are no prizes for guessing how it came by its name and certainly it is a marvellous sight at the end of a day's play to note just how many enormous sacks of empty beer cans have been accumulated over five or six hours. The Voice of Cans Corner is a character called Ian Donnelly. I had been speaking for approximately thirty seconds of my first commentary spell when a voice worthy of Stentor himself interrupted from just 20 yards away: 'What about the seagalls? Tell us about the seagalls. Henry Blowjob doesn't talk about the crickut, he talks about the flyming seagalls. What're you on about?' (It is perhaps unnecessary to explain that Henry Blofeld had been there on a previous occasion, and to *Test Match Special* listeners it will be similarly superfluous to mention that Henry enjoys a certain preoccupation with matters ornithological during commentary, not to mention buses, helicopters and the Post Office Tower. Now read on.) In a commentary box the microphones are designed to catch the voice directed into them and to eliminate all other sounds as far as possible. The sound effects of bat on ball and of the crowd are picked up by entirely different mikes and these are fed behind the commentator's voice at a volume which is strictly monitored by an engineer. Although my earphones were supposed to soundproof me from extraneous noise (thus avoiding distractions, for commentary — no less than playing the game — is a matter of concentration) the voice of Ian Donnelly, for 'twas none other, came very clearly *through* the headphones. It also came over the effects mike, down the line and *into* my headphones, almost taking my head off before the engineers could balance the sound. This was something I had never encountered before and for the next 20 minutes or so it was a bit of a struggle. When a voice is directing questions at you from very close range geographically and even closer quarters in the electronic sense, it is very difficult not to answer them. I tried the odd throw-away line to my inquisitor — which would have had the effect of making listeners in Wellington, Christchurch and points south wonder what the hell I was talking about — but IT, in the person of Stentor, would not go away. At the end of my first commentary stint in New Zealand I felt as though I had done ten rounds with Mohammed Ali. What was worse was that I knew it had been a *terrible* 20 minutes of commentary.

Dejectedly, I went out of the box to sit in the sunshine on the opposite side from Cans Corner where there were some unoccupied seats. Suddenly I didn't like New Zealand quite so much and it was quite certain that on the evidence of their first 20 minutes of me, the people of New Zealand were not going to be too taken with the visiting commentator, either. I was vaguely conscious that someone had taken a seat somewhere close to me but, deep in the pit of self-pity, I didn't look up until a voice asked, 'You the Pom commentator?' Miserably, I confessed and then, recognising that hated voice, I turned on the substantial person of Mr Ian Donnelly and accused, 'And you're the so-and-so who's been barracking me for the last twenty minutes.' 'Barracking — how's that? Aw, cam awn. You can take a little shout, can't you? Like a beer?' Icily, more icily than any beer that ever came out of one of his cans, I dismissed my tormentor: 'I don't drink when I am working.' Utterly unmoved by my adoption of the nearest I can get to a BBC accent (if such exists these days) Mr Donnelly shrugged it off: 'Suit yourself.' And he went back to Cans Corner. During my next commentary period he and his flock — there are many and they all have loud voices — left me strictly alone and perversely I now panicked at the thought that I was now classified as another whingeing Pom. There was only one thing for it. I was obviously not going to beat 'em — I had better join 'em.

At luncheon I declined the invitation from my colleagues to join them for a meal on the other side of the ground and walked slowly, and exceedingly nervously, down the steps to Cans Corner. Mr Donnelly rose amidst the multitude, performed 65 introductions in the space of 15 seconds (thus avoiding the wastage of good drinking time) and handed me a can. By close of play the commentary had become a little less disciplined and bonds of friendship down below had been strengthened to a remarkable degree. They are stronger than ever today.

Don Mosey *The Best Job in the World* (1985)

Mosey's experience turns the spotlight on another contributor to cricket's rich tapestry — the spectator. Cynics say that New Zealand cricket has two types of spectator: those who go to one-day games and those who go to real matches. This is an exaggeration, for every one-day crowd includes a good proportion of people who are keenly interested in tests and first-class games as well. But one-day cricket certainly has its own atmosphere — more colourful, less retrained. Banners festoon the railings, beer tents bulge at the seams and polite applause is drowned by waves of noisy barracking. The crowd that gathered at Eden Park for New Zealand's match against England, on 19 February 1983, enjoyed themselves in typical one-day fashion.

England were batting. The word filtered through the crowd as clouds of cigarette smoke swept down the terraces. The New Zealanders entered the arena. They had been having one or two problems. Richard Hadlee, their champion strike bowler, was hamstrung and could not play. Nor could the flu-ridden John Wright, scorer of most New Zealand runs in the Benson and Hedges World Series. Many New Zealanders felt distinctly uneasy about such defections. However, Glenn Turner, the master, was there, playing his first home game for his country in all of six years. And it was reassuring to know that in Bruce Edgar, New Zealand had a courageous fighter to slot into the top order.

The atmosphere of the one-day cricket match pervades. The crowd hums expectantly, incessantly. Tavare and, somewhat surprisingly, Botham open the batting. The beginning is deliberate and watchful, but Tavare loses his leg stump to one of Cairns's uncanny in-swingers. A swinging yorker, in fact. England are 1 for 17.

The crowd react in a variety of ways. Toasts are offered and accepted. Much noise is engendered. A serious-looking husband can be seen explaining to his wife the affects of adverse humidity on the movement of a cricket ball. She finally accepts the scientific theory of magic as the only possible cause. A scantily clad young thing wants to know if a 'swinging yorker' is a Jim Dandy from the city of York.

Botham, looking to get on with it, is fetched an eye-watering blow in the vitals. As he gropes and grovels, much whispering between wives and husbands and boyfriends and girlfriends is set in motion. Those in the know roar their heads off and spare not a smidgen of sympathy for Botham. It's all good-natured stuff, although a sign in the crowd proclaiming that 'Botham takes it up the Bottom', serves as a reminder that one-day cricket can also attract another sort of aficionado.

David Gower, the left-hander who turns batting into an art form, is at the crease now, and although he looks untroubled, he is having problems with his timing. A bit of fine tuning, one suspects, and he will be away on us again. No English batsman enjoys New Zealand bowling as much as Gower.

'Gower Power is turning sour', announces another sign in the crowd. The prophecy may be right, for Gower is certainly being tied down. Suddenly things begin happening at the other end. Botham offers a catch to Morrison at mid-on and Morrison, with measured calm, accepts it. The crowd erupts. Botham, a potential pugilist, has gone. The 'Nice one Morrison' sign is hoisted on the terraces. 40 for 2. At the same score Lamb and Gower fluff their lines and Lamb, anything but a meek and mild batsman, is run out. At 40 for 3 the home crowd begin crowing, but Gower and Randall bat sensibly to secure the England hundred.

During the drinks break the crowd noise continues unabated. Norman Cowans, England's twelfth man, can be seen doing wheelies in the motorised drinks trolley. A rather caustic voice postulates that if it had been the Australian twelfth man he would have attempted to side-swipe Glenn Turner. Another, equally caustic, believes the West Indies twelfth man would have run [umpire] Fred Goodall over.

Chatfield is now bowling as dry as the throats of the patrons. The occasional ball is keeping low. Finally Chatfield rattles Randall's stumps as Randall ducks around like he's dodging machine gun fire. The raucous crowd appreciate Randall's antics. The roar of New Zealand supporters. That was the missing ingredient in the Benson and Hedges matches.

Randall's 30 runs have been invaluable to the England cause and this is highlighted when Trevor Jesty holes out to a jovial Jeremy Coney. England are in the doldrums. The crowd is completely transported, swept up in the excitement engendered by their own performance, as much as that of their cricket team. Gower is still there. Damn the man.

The turning-point arrives as Snedden digs one in just short of a length. Gower, his timing still awry, skies the ball miles into the air. In the old days a distinct hush would descend over a cricket crowd at such a time. The hush would owe its existence as much to a collective unwillingness to put the potential catcher off his catch, as to a genuine, collective apprehension that the catch would not be secured. Times have changed and Morrison, the man designated by fate to pit himself against the miscue, was afforded a deafening roar. Morrison, usually a phlegmatic sort, senses the occasion too and there is a feeling of tremendous tension as the ball hovers above the pitch. Finally his fingers close hungrily around the ball and in relief he tumbles backwards. Gower has gone. The end for England is nigh. The 'I don't believe it' sign flutters in the crowd.

Gould, Miller, Jackman and Willis are dismissed for a total of 11 runs. Only Marks of the lower-order England batsmen is able to fathom the pitch or beat the field. With each dismissal the crowd becomes more and more delirious. It is a carnival now and well-known local cricket identities circulate. Lord Ted filters through the crowd, spreading goodwill and a certain amount of beer amongst his subjects. Gareth Bean, the barracker's barracker, is going through his routine with renewed gusto. One-time winner of the 'Cricket Watcher of the Year' award, he has a distinct ritual, and a jaunty brown attaché case that set him apart from the average supporter. After each ball is bowled Gareth, in strict sequence, takes a drink from a range of beverages assembled in miniature bottles, hurls an observation — sometimes pithy, sometimes hackneyed — at the players, and then makes an entry in his diary. After which the attaché case is closed to await the bowling of the next ball…

One of the problems, or delights, of one-day cricket is that every over, almost every delivery is significant. Not like test match cricket where if you're half an hour late getting to the park, chances are that little of significance has been squandered. A number of spectators at Eden Park on 19 February were late resuming their seats at the commencement of the New Zealand innings. Some were tied up in pie queues and latrine tents until the end of the third over. In that time Glenn Turner had bludgeoned five boundaries. Turner's thunderous start in effect represented the winning of the game. Some of his shots were electrifying, particularly those despatched through the off-side field. Once a rigid purist, he was now prepared to expose his stumps in order to create space to execute his flat-bat cuts and drives. His display was a timely reminder to new and born-again cricket fans that the ball did not have to be heaved out of the park by local blacksmiths in order to keep the meter ticking over.

With the ball not coming on to the bat with any great pace, Turner displayed remarkable timing. Edgar chipped in with some cultured shots too and the New Zealand hundred came up with both openers still at the crease. Lance Cairns was promoted to first drop and he was greeted by a tumultuous noise from the crowd when the first wicket fell. A couple of decent hoicks over the ropes and 19 runs later Cairns was departing the scene, the New Zealand cause materially assisted by his efforts. Although Jeff Crowe was lbw to Botham for 15, it remained a simple matter for Howarth and Coney to accumulate the remaining handful of runs required to secure victory.

The winning runs. Millions of kids invade the pitch. God knows where they're going or what they hope to retrieve. A sea of humanity, a subsiding cauldron of sound. The carnival is over. Time to try to find your jandals and other sundries. Time to try to negotiate the swirling tides of spectators, with throbbing temples and slumbering legs.

'What's lbw, Dad?' a small boy asks his father.

'I'll explain it when we got home, son.'

Beer cans clatter, kids gripe. A struggling yobbo is escorted away…

Back in the now silent canyons of Eden Park typewriters clatter in the press box. Several flaked fans have to be aroused and driven from their beer-can beds. Beer cans rise in great mountains. One corner of the ground is knee-deep in cans. Rubbish and cast-offs. Officials scratch their heads. The cricket circus was in town.

Graham Hutchins *The Howarth Years* (1985)

Another tour, another international against England, this time against Graham Gooch's 1991 England team — and a reporter from Wellington's *Evening Post* braves the Basin Reserve's infamous bank. This is where one-day cricket gets its bad name; where being a spectator is to be part of a gladiatorial contest, with no-one quite sure who will be thrown to the lions next.

The distant thwack of leather on willow mingles with the steady slurp of beer from a hundred polystyrene cups. The England innings is underway. Not a lot is happening to give much hope of a Kiwi win.

As usual, bringing cans into the ground is banned. Beer is sold at $3 per 500 ml cup. The queues stretch forever.

The fans in and around the middle of three canvas tents on the embankment are hunkering down for what promises to be a long, humid and thirsty afternoon.

Then without warning it is all on. One of those incidents the television commentators usually refer to as 'a bit of a disturbance up on the bank'. They leave it to the viewers' imagination to fill in the details.

I am about 5 metres away, but can't see how it starts. Everyone else in the vicinity apparently does and subsequently they relate their conflicting versions to the police.

What I do see is two men having a punch-up near the tent flap. Because of the slope they tumble down the grass bank, cutting a swathe through fans, blankets, chilly bins, deck chairs and lunch boxes.

The crowd on either side leap up for a better view. Or to avoid getting trampled. Those further away who can't see what is going on cheer anyway.

The police at these sorts of events go into a hovering mode. This involves strolling about on the fringes chatting amiably, while keeping an eye out for troublemakers.

There must have been bad vibes in the air. Before the pair can do much damage they disappear under a blue wave.

Mike Atherton takes a single from a prod to square leg but who notices?

Those near the tent put their gear back together, brush themselves down and refocus on what else is going on. Some even look at the cricket.

The fans, many with faces painted with lurid fluoro sunblock, regard the whole thing as part of the entertainment. The police are less amused. They are having 'a serious talk' with one of the pair in the fight. The other stands with his mates dabbing a bleeding lip with his singlet.

Various witnesses offer their version of events to any of the half dozen police who had rapidly materialised with the first flurry of action.

They invariably begin. 'Well, I suppose you realise you've got the wrong guy…'

To sort out precisely what happened would take the wisdom of Solomon. As they talk everyone cools down. The police eventually send one of the combatants to another part of the ground.

Meanwhile, this incident, which took about 30 minutes to resolve, is history for the fans on the bank.

While New Zealand are still struggling to get into the game other things are occupying them, none of them novel to one-day cricket crowds. Like chanting at anyone brave enough to walk in front of them. The usual advice: 'Get your gear off!' 'Get your tie off!' etc…

Pommie bashing is in vogue, as the upper-order English batsmen grind their way to what looks like an inevitable win.

It is mostly good-natured.

One English fan carries the battle to the enemy. He sports an English rugby jersey and scarf. He taunts the crowd by waving the flag of St George at them and pointing at the scoreboard.

He is showered with rubbish and insults but thrives on the reaction…

The nature of barracking at cricket matches has changed with the advent of one-day cricket.

Long days at test cricket were enlivened by a few spectators with loud voices and penetrating wit. They were often genuinely funny. Now it's all mass chanting, seldom original.

As in this game, until the avalanche of English wickets in the last 30 minutes fires up the crowd, the cricket often seems irrelevant.

The emphasis is on having a good time, a few laughs and a day out.

The scrap earlier and a few other similar dust-ups through the afternoon are handled in a low-key way by the police who had a few laughs themselves. At one stage a man in an English soccer shirt who had been removed from the ground was being photographed on the footpath outside the Basin before being put in the paddy wagon to cool off.

Watching the 'scene' from the embankment was a dishevelled tearaway who had himself narrowly missed being kicked out.

He sidled up to a policeman and patted him on the back: 'It's about time you kicked that guy out — he's a right stirrer!'

The policeman grins, gives him a 'there but for the grace of God go you' look and wanders on.

The final pulsating minutes mean the bank crowd can forget about building polystyrene pipes out of beer cups and the other distractions. They get right behind Martin Crowe and his team, generating a massive volume of noise.

If the Kiwis hadn't snatched a fairy tale victory the fans would still have gone away happy.

The win is the froth on their lager. A day on the bank is a happening which doesn't necessarily depend for its success on the home team winning or, apparently, even knowing where you are.

As I go out the gate one of the bank fans I had met earlier spots me.

'What a day mate,' he beams. 'You know, I've lived in Wellington now for 11 years and this is the first time I've ever been to Athletic Park.'

Barry Hawkins 'Among the Fans on the Basin's Bank', *Evening Post* 25 June 1991

A cricket match brings together many elements. The atmosphere of the venue, the skills of the players, the attitude of the crowd and the efforts of umpires, scorers and commentators, all contribute to the drama that unfolds. It is in the test match arena that this amalgam of elements is seen at its most unpredictable. On 22 February 1990, the opening day of a test between New Zealand and India was highjacked by New Zealand's wicketkeeper, Ian Smith, with a whirlwind innings of 173 off 136 balls. It was the highest score ever achieved by a number nine batsman. Not content with this, the belligerent Smith struck Atul Wassan for 2, 4, 4, 2, 6 and 6 off successive balls, to equal the test record for the most runs by one batsman in an over.

Nothing in the morning's play had suggested the batting blitz to come, but that is the fascination of cricket. When all the elements gel it can be, as writer Peter Calder found out on that February day, more than the players and more than just a game.

 For all of our species has made a fearful mess of this planet, there are some things we have done right.

Visitors from another galaxy, picking through the debris of our failed civilisation a few million years hence will not conclude that our time was utterly misspent.

For locked in a time capsule somewhere will be the evidence of the truly great achievements we managed during the blink in time we were in charge of planet Earth.

That curious hand will marvel at Handel's *Messiah*, at *King Lear*, at glossy colour photographs of the Sistine Chapel's ceiling and at the 10-speed bicycle.

And — since they will be, by definition, a civilisation far more refined and sophisticated than our own — they will stand in awe before that sublime, deliciously variegated, infinitely versatile invention known as a cricket test.

The drama in five acts on which the curtain rose at Eden Park in Auckland on Thursday has already been staged countless times on myriad grounds around the world.

But this, like all other cricket matches, had no script and even the most literate watcher of the unfolding action could never rob the next line of its surprise.

There is no magic like the opening day of a cricket test and the two or three thousand devotees at the park for the opening ball on Thursday know the magic well.

The pulse quickens long before the game even begins as the keen spectators ascend the steps from the drab promenades behind the stands to take up vantage points around the ground.

The lush outfield springs into view like an unexpected sunrise. Its grass is neatly mown into checkerboard squares and the small brownish rectangle at its centre, roped off like a boxing ring before a prize-fight, awaits — passive and patient — the unlocking of its secret fortunes.

As the spectators unpack cushions and vacuum flasks, spread crumpled morning newspapers on their knees and settle in, the atmosphere is scarcely one of excitement. So stark an emotion belongs to later in the day, when there are deeds to applaud, odds to be weighed, hopes to be raised or dashed.

It is more a sense of quiet anticipation that runs through the folk lucky or wily enough to have dodged other responsibilities to sit in one spot for the next seven hours and watch the game go from newborn to toddler.

They greet each other like old friends meeting at a family gathering. Their presence is taken for granted, their common purpose presupposed, and there are a few minutes to compare notes on children's ages, business fortunes and holiday highlights.

Many conversations turn to the prospect of a result in the game. This is not a crowd to be puzzled or exasperated by the notion that 22 men can battle six hours a day for five days in the blistering sun at a game which, more often than not, produces neither a winner nor a loser.

Eden Park would never rank as one of the world's more picturesque cricket grounds. No willows weep over the scoreboard, no river winds past its boundary fence, no green belt stretches away from its gates.

Instead, ill-kempt houses crowd its eastern fences and hulking, drab goods trains rumble along the hillside beyond the scoreboard.

Yet, dressed up in its finest livery for the season's first Auckland international, and with a keen crowd speckled across its seats, it looks every bit as pretty as it should.

Like all true objects of beauty, it reveals its splendour from all angles.

On the south-east terrace, which will this morning fill early and this afternoon bear witness to scenes of less-than-dignified enthusiasm, only a few scattered spectators set up camp on the hard rails of seats.

But the view from the area which in the late '70s was branded the Richard Hadlee stand (after its occupants' penchant for rhythmically chanting the name of New Zealand's fast bowler) is one no hard-bitten fan would trade for an acre of shade and a cool lime and soda.

Meanwhile, high on the south stand, more privileged patrons recline in the comfort of the 28 hospitality boxes. It's the first cricket season since the plush, well-appointed boxes were completed and plenty of collar-and-tie middle-management types are enjoying the chance to play authorised hooky from their office duties.

Their enthusiasm is well-oiled by liberal quantities of the hospitality and their appreciation of the players' feats is expressed in throaty roars that would nicely fit the terraces.

In box number 14 — the one set aside for honoured guests and past and present officials of the park's management — the ambience is more restrained.

Old hands, who were witness to New Zealand's first test win — on this ground in 1956 against the formidable West Indies — watch from their high-tech eyrie, with the supreme composure of those who know that one test match is simply a bar in the symphony of the game.

Mervyn Wallace, the vice-captain of a pre-war New Zealand side which was led by Richard Hadlee's father Walter, enthuses in an undertone, conscious that he should not interrupt other's enjoyment of the match.

'There's nothing quite like the first morning of a test match.' he says. 'Not for the general public perhaps (this with a connoisseur's delight but not a trace of superciliousness). It's just a very interesting time.'

He will not allow that this morning's first session has been a good deal too interesting, with five of his countrymen having been sent, drooping and dejected, back to the pavilion and the score — a sad 78 — lower than the All Blacks have been known to rack up.

He won't even be drawn into criticism of the batsman's efforts, other than to say that 'it's not what you hit, it's what you leave that makes you a great batsman.'

It is an ancient wisdom which, by the end of the day, the stroppy Ian Smith will have shown himself never to have heard.

For the five days of a cricket match, Eden Park becomes home to a small community.

Between the two extremes — the rowdies on the terraces and the old gladiators dreaming of distant skirmishes — all manner of spectators ring the perimeter, united by nothing other than their common passion for the game.

Matrons purl another few stitches for beloved grandchildren as the bowler returns to his mark. Small boys cluster at the boundary rope near the end of each session, their bats clutched in sweaty hopeful hands, bracing themselves for the sudden dash on to the arena where they will thrust it at a thirsty player and pray for an autograph on its scarred blade.

The crowd is dotted with the dark and delighted faces of the city's Indian community, here to give the tourists a hometown welcome.

By the time this first day is over there will be more records than those without pen and notepaper can keep track of.

The record for the most runs in a test over will be matched. New Zealand and ninth-wicket partnerships marks will be passed and an 80-odd-year record for a number nine batsman will be battered into second place.

They are moments which the faithful will savour, as their predecessors in the stands and terraces savoured earlier memorable days.

Today will join the day when Walter Hammond scored 295 runs in a day on this ground — a feat beaten only by the great Don Bradman.

Today will be remembered alongside Rodney Redmond's and Mark Greatbatch's debut test centuries and Bruce Taylor's 30-minute half century — still history's third equal fastest.

For much of the morning, it looked like being remembered — or preferably forgotten — alongside our 1955 effort, when we were bowled out for a miserly total of 26.

But for most of those who took their places in Eden Park on Thursday morning — and who will be there again today — what happens out in the middle is almost — just almost — of no consequence.

Test cricket matches can be won or lost, fast or slow, full of action or threaded through with subtleties that only the aficionado will appreciate.

One thing they must not be is missed.

Peter Calder 'King Lear, Michelangelo — and Smithy', **New Zealand Herald**

24 February 1990

FIVE

CATCHING THE SPIRIT

It is hard to define the spirit of cricket without sounding sentimental or high-flown. Those who are passionate about the game have no need to explain it to themselves — although they sometimes try to put it into words, if only to show others what they are missing. The poet and novelist, Elizabeth Smither, conveys something of the dedicated cricket lover's feeling and fascination for the game in one of her short stories. The main character in the story, Victoria, has loved cricket since childhood. She goes to as many matches as she can and, since hearing the flamboyant English writer and broadcaster, Henry 'Blowers' Blofeld, on *Sports' Roundup,* has dreamed of being a commentator. Instead, she becomes engaged to Peter, who does not share her enthusiasm and finds it difficult to understand.

Victoria and Peter go to several cricket matches: New Zealand versus Pakistan, Central Districts versus Zimbabwe. After a while it becomes clear that Peter will not go to a full test match. He will come for an innings — when Crowe is batting for instance — or part of the final day. He simply cannot spare the time, he tells Victoria. 'What did I miss?' he asks later, and she cannot tell him. That Greatbatch went out while she was buying a can of

Steinlager, that nothing happened for hours and then there were two runouts. It is impossible to explain the philosophy of cricket to Peter, who now he has engaged her interest in himself, listens less. In future, she sees, he will regard it as a peccadillo. 'Victoria is crazy about cricket, you know. And not the one-dayers either. Those dreadful five-dayers where nothing happens.'

Nonetheless, over dinner, Victoria does try to convince him for the last time.

'It's not that nothing happens,' she begins.

'Compared to other sports,' he interrupts.

'True,' says Victoria, biting her lip.

'We're talking of five-day tests here,' he confirms, like a man checking his watch.

'How can I make you understand?' Victoria groans. 'You're already prejudiced against them.'

'White men on a green field. Leather on willow,' he goes on, taking some of her best lines.

'Damn you,' says Victoria.

'Well?' says Peter.

'I feel as though I am watching my life unfold. The present, past and the future. I've been here before, I think.'

'You assuredly have,' says Peter.

'Don't interrupt. When I watch cricket I think of my future plans and what might become of them. I consider fate, which is something I don't normally do. I think of my chances and I adjudicate them rather slim.'

'What chances?' Peter asks impatiently.

'Any chances. My chances of anything. My chances with you for one thing.'

'I'll ignore that,' Peter replies. 'I consider that settled.'

'But don't you see, thanks to cricket, I can't. I could if it was one-day cricket. You could bowl me out or vice-versa. It wouldn't matter much one way or the other. I could always bowl you out the next time. A simple contest. Any fool could cope with that.'

'I never realised you took cricket so seriously.'

'It's not cricket, it's life itself.'

Peter thinks Victoria, wearing his sapphire and diamond ring on her finger, is exaggerating of course. He dimly recalls speech days at school where life is compared to a game and conduct to sportsmanship. Life is a game of tiddlywinks. Victoria has been overcome by philosophy, he decides. Five days sitting on the terraces is unnatural for a woman. When they are married he will restrict her to one-day matches.

But when Peter attempts to suggest this he's met with a surprising ultimatum. Victoria intends never giving up the five-day game, and what's more she won't marry him unless they can honeymoon in Melbourne where the M.C.C. are playing Australia for the Ashes.

One hope Victoria has consigned to oblivion: she will never be a lady cricket commentator. She will leave that to Blowers and lesser men. Blowers understands that 'it isn't cricket' with all its meanings is still important. And that 'cricket has always had something to do with all that is decent in life'.

As for herself and Peter, they are still negotiating. Two days at the M.C.G. is all he will allow so far. But Victoria is determined. 'Everything will be all right, you'll see,' he says, but already he sounds slightly weary, as if he has doubts. How many seasoned test cricketers have felt the same.

'My dear old thing,' says Victoria.

Elizabeth Smither 'Cricket' *Metro* March 1995

Great players are an important part of cricket's history but they do not necessarily hold the key to the spirit of the game — at least, not in the opinion of one of New Zealand's most resolute test openers, John Wright.

The bonds that hold 11 individuals together and make them a team are forged in the changing room. If you've got a good spirit there, the side will tick and work as a team. You take your dressing room spirit onto the field and if the guys are unhappy there, it will show on the park. Any team has its stars, then its bread and butter players, and finally the guys who perhaps aren't quite good enough to hold down a regular place. Often it's the third category — the blokes sometimes called the dirt trackers — who can make people laugh, at themselves and others, and who mould everyone together. Every team has to have these sort of characters. They do the same job in club, first-class and international cricket. Often their role isn't recognised but they're worth their weight in gold, espcially to managers and captains.

Dirt trackers can laugh at themselves: Gary Robertson has played one test — against Australia in 1985 — and taken one wicket for 91. After Dipak Patel got his first test wicket in Perth [during the 1987–88 series], Robbo sidled up to him and said 'congratulations, you've finally caught up with me'.

Dirt trackers come into their own when you're in strife. They have a philosophical approach to life which enables them to put things in perspective. Robin Penharrow, a leg spinner who played for Northern Districts, personified this attitude: the first time he got picked for Poverty Bay, he turned up with his girlfriend and fishing rod but forgot his boots.

The other thing about these guys is that they make playing the game enjoyable. All the statistics and achievements that the public and the media fuss about pale into insignificance in the end; what I remember — and it's the same for everyone who relates to people — are the guys I've played with. It's the same whether you're an international or a club cricketer — there's something about guys who get off their butts and away from the TV and go to play on a Saturday afternoon. You've still got to get the selectors' nod of course: my mate Harry reckons the only reason he gets picked for an Auckland musicians' social team is that his wife makes a great bacon and egg pie.

John Wright with Paul Thomas *Christmas in Rarotonga* (1990)

The spirit of cricket burns strongly in those who play the game badly, but persist in turning out, week after week, because they enjoy it so much.

No passing parade of New Zealand cricketers could end without reference to the most important of them all. His name has never appeared in *Wisden*, his career batting average looks much more impressive after the decimal point than before it — he has it worked out to four places — his bowling is usually limited to about two overs on the last day of each season, and his fielding consists largely of posthumous little pounces at the ball, like a short-sighted butterfly hunter.

He is the below average cricketer, and there are many of him. But he is more important to the game than the most eminent test player or the most authoritative administrator. Without him, the game would not survive, because it would be meaningless.

He began his cricket career when he was four, making scythe-like sweeps on the back lawn with a sawn-off bat. This hint of the rural in his style has survived years of reading about the techniques of the game as expounded by its masters, hours of intensive practice before full-length mirrors, and the advice of a long succession of expert coaches, each one of whom ultimately took refuge in abuse, or alcohol, or both.

At secondary school there were sufficient teams for him to find a place in the lowest, and it was there that his cricket reached its climax. A casual reference to acquaintance with someone who knew a cousin of a New Zealand player gave him the leadership of the team, which allowed him a full and glorious summer of blissful theorising with his players. He read and re-read Jardine on captaincy, he spent hours drawing diagrams of field placings to fit any conceivable set of circumstances, and his team's defeats were usually by an innings. But each disappointment bred another theory to overcome it.

After leaving school he joined a club, and his place in the lowest team was really secure only during the weeks other carefree souls might be spending a holiday at the beach with their families. He remembers his wedding day well, because of the Saturday's cricket it cost him. All this time he read cricket, talked cricket, spent whole nights crouched over the radio while tests were on overseas, and ultimately, with tremendous pride, accepted the office of club assistant-secretary.

There was a wonderful day when, through some whimsy of his captain, he went in at number eight, and thus had a few minutes to watch his club's first side. The senior captain, casting about desperately for replacements for those who had left to attend weddings or were suffering from fibrositis, noticed the familiar figure of the below-average cricketer and with some misgivings asked him to field for a while.

This was intoxicating success, and he could hardly be blamed for his excitement. But the umpire at square leg, a venerable old gentleman enjoying the afternoon sunshine and wondering whether his asparagus bed might not be the better for another application of salt, found it hard to forgive the fast under-arm throw which took him in the small of the back. But there was a magnificent catch a little later, clutched to the midriff with arms and elbows and all. That really made the day.

After retiring from senior cricket, the below average cricketer concentrated on helping those in the lower grades. Never anything but modest, he was still willing to give advice to those who sought it, and to his sons, who didn't. He continued to work for the club, he hardly ever missed a practice, and he learned not to be too much out of countenance when he was bowled three times on end by some fresh-faced little angel wheeling up leg-breaks. He saved his holidays so they would give him time to see every important match, and many which were not.

Now he has put on a little weight, his hair is greying and he peers hopefully down the pitch, after an elaborate taking of guard, through spectacles. He finds it more difficult now to advance his right foot, with which he has these last few summers intercepted most of the firmer hits which have come his way.

But he plays on, and only last summer reached double figures, with the assistance of a couple of leg-byes which somehow found their way into the line above their place in the score-book. He is a kind but firm critic of players and selectors, and there is a whisper that he will be made a life member of his club. Not for him the glories of a test match century, tours overseas, hair tonic advertisements, and talent money. But he does not complain. He still tries desperately hard. He still feels it is a privilege to play.

R.T. Brittenden *New Zealand Cricketers* (1961)

Today, Brittenden's 'below-average cricketer' has many friends. They are just as keen on the game and have a much greater range of outlets for their enthusiasm.

Cricket is a bit like country music in that I always knew it would come right. There was a time not so long ago when I felt a bit ashamed to admit I owned half a dozen Kris Kristofferson, Jerry Jeff Walker and Amazing Rhythm Aces albums. Now, in Ponsonby and Grey Lynn, everyone has Lyall Lovett, Randy Travis and Steve Earle CDs and they don't hesitate to let it be known how hip they are.

It's the same with cricket. There was a time when only boys from the city's 'top' schools played cricket; when the Eden Park stands were deserted during a test match. That was before television and the one-day game. Now the whole country stays up after midnight in January to watch a largely meaningless but hugely exciting 50-over match coming in from the Melbourne Cricket Ground, and one-day games at Eden Park are regularly pre-sold to 40,000 people.

I'm talking here about relatively elegant cricket (although the last 10 overs of a one-day game, when a run chase is on, can get decidedly low on finesse). For the most part, the game's revival has been in the area of coarse cricket, which is what you see on Saturdays and Sundays at a hundred suburban grounds as you drive by on the way to the beach or the garden centre. It is characterised by player-umpires, pitches of infinite variety, occasionally eccentric dress (by Lord's standards), and great enthusiasm.

Coarse cricket engages me at four levels. Over the winter a team from *Metro* plays indoor cricket — the coarsest type of all — in a mixed league at Glenfield. Indoor cricket is fast, exciting and can be dangerous. It has very little to do with the real game, and with its slog and run like hell approach can, in fact, ruin your real game. But it's also quite addictive, and although I keep saying I'm going to give it up, I never do.

In the past year, I have found myself on Saturday mornings out in the middle umpiring in places as diverse as Edgewater College and Westlake Boys' High School as my 14-year-old's 6B4 team has struggled to emulate his school's old boys, Greatbatch and the Crowes. They're all keen and try hard, and I enjoy their company and their enthusiasm. They win as many as they lose.

Then, on Saturday afternoons — sometimes after a high-speed drive across the city — you'll find me at mid-on at Devonport Domain number three for the North Shore club's president's grade team.

I'm probably out of my depth with these guys, many of whom are former top players who have lost few of their skills, and when people ask me whether I bat or bowl I have to answer truthfully that I field. As I write this, my talents with the bat have so far this season yielded scores of 8, 8, 0 and 2.

The North Shore game, though, is the high point of my cricket week, and if, at 43, there is still improvement in me — which I am coming to increasingly doubt — keeping my place in this team will provide the incentive to get better.

Finally, after sleeping the exhausted sleep of the just on summer Saturday nights, I turn out on Sundays for the Champagne Cricket Club, a group of splendid fellows who work in trades as diverse as restaurateurism, medicine and the law. At Stanley Bay Park, under scarlet pohutukawa; with wives and lovers, children and dogs; we spread rugs and Sunday papers, open picnic hampers and settle down for a fine day's cricket against teams with names like the Antiquarians and Extended Players.

This is entirely different from the previous day's game. For one thing, I am allowed to bowl, and from time to time I manage to take a wicket or three, although the skills of batting still largely elude me. My wife says I'm probably blind, and I'm inclined to think she could be right.

The Champagners and our opponents epitomise coarse cricket. Through us runs the common thread of hope. None of us are youths, but we all know with certainty that we've still got what it takes, that if we can one day get our run-up right, get that rhythm going, we'll get wickets consistently; that if we can beat the fear, we'll get runs.

For my part, I know for sure that if I can only stay at the wicket for quarter of an hour and get my eye in, I'll get my confidence back. Until I do, I know exactly how Jeff Crowe felt last summer when, virtually runless, he was dropped from the New Zealand team. That's what keeps me going, week in, week out through summer — the tantalisation. As 5 p.m. Friday comes around, all over town thousands of coarse cricketers are sharing my fear and my dream.

Warwick Roger 'Coarse Cricket' **Metro** February 1989

Roger's 'coarsest cricket of all', indoor cricket, is a striking illustration of the game's capacity to reinvent itself in new forms, so that it continues to gather devotees.

I used to play indoor cricket long before the current boom — in the living room with a practice golf ball and the test commentary turned up full. On my home pitch I became expert at picking up the line of the delivery early against the regency stripe background and with head down and left elbow extended in textbook style I would graft my way to my first 50. As my one-handed bowling began to tire I would step up the scoring rate, going right back onto the hearth rug to whip the ball away behind the sofa for four or lift it over the footstool at silly mid-on and into the passage for six. I was not just a batsman, though. I mixed late outswing with very sharp pace from my four-pace run (short not so much to get me through a long, hard season as to give me a full 10 foot of pitch to follow-through on). It was a rare over in which I didn't whip one through the batsman's defences and shatter the fire-irons. The only thing missing was spectators, or at least fellow-players, to witness the triumphs.

For that it was necessary to play outside with a hard ball that came from further away, but much faster, and with an evil fizzing sound. The nonchalant living-room flick for four became a nervous prod accompanied by all-too-frequent shouts of glee from fielders who were considerably more agile and aggressive than the furniture. Progress was possible, but all that remained of the casual grace was a repertoire of habits — surveying the field, tugging at the batting gloves, adjusting the cap, tapping the bat rhythmically on the ground.

In the kind of indoor cricket played nightly in dozens of empty wool-stores and warehouses around the country there is no time or patience for such little niceties. It is the kind of cricket you get on Eden Park or the Basin Reserve — between innings and in the lunch-break. The kind of noisy, non-stop game played on thousands of back lawns and against the back wall of the bike sheds. Some of those who play it are every bit as convinced as I ever was that they are Lillee or Sobers. Others have never even heard of them.

The game is played in teams of eight (most often office or social club teams), mixed at the lower, non-competition levels but tending to sexual seg-regation and macho overtones when the results start to count. Everybody in every team gets to bowl two overs and to bat for four overs — guaranteed. If you are dismissed while batting your team loses some of its total and you bat on. This raises the definite possibility of finishing an innings with a negative score, something not even the New Zealand national team in its darkest days has had to worry about.

The fielders are arrayed around a carpeted cage of fishing nets a little longer and considerably wider than the usual cricket practice net. Just like my living room, run-ups are of limited length although the pitch is a full 22 yards long. The ball looks like the real thing, but is actually a tennis ball encased in leather. The bats are real and the wickets, although of regulation dimensions, are made of aluminium and make a sound very like the fire-irons when they are shattered. Runs are scored in a more or less conventional way, with players only having to run half the length of the pitch and net boundaries scoring two or four.

The result is a quick-fire game with a winner decided in little more than an hour and a half. People of widely differing skills can be accommodated with a number of ad hoc rules. Bowlers (especially women bowlers) who have never been taught the fine points dividing bowling from throwing are not no-balled (unless too successful) and those who cannot muster the length even with that liberal definition are permitted to deliver the ball from halfway down the pitch. There is a single umpire, most often provided by the organ-isers, perched above the end of the net. The umpire's duties include ruling on run-outs and other dismissals, policing the regulations and keeping track of the rapidly fluctuating scores.

The social games are raucous and sometimes ribald, with little note being taken of the score and little worry about the standard of performance of team-mates. As the competition hots up the general jeering and unsolicited advice of the casual games is replaced by a lot of grunting and appeals of test-match fervour. Pink-faced men in football shorts which probably fitted them better last winter fling themselves around alarmingly and come up with an injury you won't get at Lord's — carpet burn.

The steam builds up under the floodlights and the games end with players in the kind of lather you might expect to see after a squash or basketball game. The lighthearted ones debate the merits of pizzas first or straight to the pub. The competitors congratulate their opponents with the malicious heartiness of those who are sure they've been robbed, before retiring to dab on the mercurochrome and add up batting averages in their heads. The owners of the venue look at booking charts filled a month or more in advance at $80 a game and do some rather more satisfying arithmetic.

Frank Stark 'Yes, but is it cricket?', *New Zealand Listener* 11 August 1984

There is a strong spiritual dimension to another form of cricket found extensively in New Zealand, particularly in Auckland.

Grey Lynn wakes to another day of kilikti...parratta tat tat, parratta tat tat, tat...the slow rolling clatter of sticks against cabinbread tins. A lazy jazz-time beat, for the gathering heat of a summer morning, drifts over the hollows and ridges of what could be anywhere in the Pacific.

Other drummers, given to solemn poundings, join the cabinbread beat with big bass marching drums. Church elders, deacons and various other functionaries of lesser stripe, like heavy-throated bulls roaring across a paddock, vie through distorting loudspeakers to call to the assembling flock. The sweet swell of extraordinary choral singing rises with the sun — a sound pushed from the body with almost electronic purity and control. Already there is dancing. It is a perfect day.

Within a few hours Grey Lynn Park, traditionally the haunt of solitary men walking their dogs, has been transformed into an island of tropical vibrance and charm. The suburb (who was Grey? What was Lynn?) takes to the new mood with surprising grace for a place still bearing the evidence of its English working-class origins. Back a hundred years, refugees from the bleak slums of England didn't have the wit to plant trees so now there aren't any, of mature size at least. But these days, gardens overflow with taro, banana palms, hibiscus — and, in the park, there is Samoan kilikiti.

You don't have to live in Grey Lynn to know at least a little about Samoan or Niuean or Tokelauan or Tongan cricket. Driving home from work, who hasn't caught a tantalising glimpse of these big strong people, wrapped in brilliant lava lavas, wielding their war-club bats in the lingering light of summer evenings?

In Nixon Park in Kingsland or next to Western Springs, in the green spaces of South Auckland and even on the Shore, what you have seen are teams practising for the end-of-year games — which stretch on for months. Every Island group has them, but it is Samoan kilikiti which overwhelms with its size, pageantry and impact — not that the palagi has ever really noticed...

Samoan cricket bears about as much resemblance to the cucumber-sandwich territory of Lord's as the sound of the word does to the English. Some, but not much. For one thing the bat — fashioned in triangular shape from the springy fau tree, decorated in gaudy splashes of colour and bound with coconut fibre — has nothing to do with the sissy wider blade of the willow. It's an out-and-out war club of such bold length that the deft flick of the shin-pad brigade is rendered impossible. A full-blooded swing and nothing else.

The ball, spun by hand from liquid rubber tapped from a living tree and compressed to rock-hard consistency, bounds down the pitch with a dangerously unpredictable velocity. Camouflaged a light gray, it twists and spins of its own accord — batting against the West Indians is rounders in comparison. You can buy both the bat and ball from Samoa House in K Road — if only for their value as artifacts.

Most Island groups play by basically the same rules; it was Samoan missionaries who, as proxies for their white masters, originally spread the game through much of the South Pacific...a side-bar to the gospel. Teams are of indefinite size — 15 a side is considered the minimum for serious competitions, 20 the maximum but, as with palagi social cricket, numbers can grow to nearer the hundred mark if the game is informal.

When the batting team reaches 35 runs, to keep the action alive, the teams swop over. Samoans, like Kerry Packer, never could warm to the endlessness of the pukka game and their rule changes pre-dated one-day cricket by a hundred years or so. The record this year was a team bowled out for 12 runs…a not inconsiderable effort given that the wickets are narrower and the caprice of the ball works equally against the bowler.

Meanwhile, back at the park, all the tents have long since been painstakingly erected, woven mats laid out in their shade — a village of nylon fale in the middle of Auckland. People are settling in for the day. Taro, pork, yam, chicken, bananas — roasted in stone umu pits the night before — have been packed neatly in baskets made from neon-bright plastic freight lashing (the kind you see washed up on beaches). Still warm in tinfoil wrapping, the food waits for the lunch break. Children ignore half-growling mothers to dip and dive before time into the iced barrels of lurid cordial already being broached by everybody.

From out in the field comes a Soweto gumboot-music rhythmic whistling. Blown from a postman's whistle, the sound sort of dives through the drum-beat, gives the cue to the fielders. One batsman has hit to the boundary and the fielders are dancing their appreciation of the skill. Samoans are big — 17 stone of proud muscle is about average — and these men are gliding their hands, their bodies, through the air with the delicacy of a Thai ballerina — rewarding the opponent with their grace.

Women's teams play on the lower field and their on-field dances run from a semi-hula to sensuous conjuring tricks of the hand. Although the women bowl underarm, if anything they whack the ball further than the men. When older women — maybe in their late fifties — take the bat it is time for wild amusement. They use the dignity of their age to come up with some outrageous humour — a wriggle there, a mad exaggerated lunge at the ball here — followed by amused bad temper. Parody is a great source of Samoan humour.

Kilikiti officials, numerous and well aware of the seriousness of their charge, all morning have been marshalling the smooth movement of teams, tabulating scores and so on. The men, in stifling suits, stand four-square in the sun for hours on end, busy not revealing the honourable pleasure of administering for the people. Behind their backs the flock, particularly women, are equally busy, deflating…a toss of the head, a sparkle in the eye, a quiet snort. The matai responsibilities of Samoan village life, though transported to an A.C.C. park in Grey Lynn, continue to weight heavily.

It was the discipline of the village structure, adapted to the urban circumstances of the new land, which brought kilikiti to the parks of Auckland in the first place — not as a sport or even as recreation (nothing as separately and neatly packaged as that). It was deliberately established here by the churches as an enduring expression of faa Samoa among the uncertainty which confronts and can paralyse any newly arrived immigrant group.

Faa Samoa is a carefully ordered living system of rules and obligations which in Auckland, particularly, finds expression through the churches; but its nature has not basically altered in thousands of years. Samoans may have been quick and adventurous in adopting the new — cricket is hardly traditional, Jesus Christ was not Samoan — but the Samoan stamp unmistakably remains. They swallowed the new; were not themselves swallowed...

So when you stroll through Grey Lynn park on kilikiti day — marvelling at the tents ringing the pitch in careful symmetry, with the silken banners; at the proliferation of organisers, the dancing, the song — what you are seeing is only the obvious stuff. At a different level, which requires deeper penetration, lies a meditative calm, a kind of security which is firmly rooted not just in Samoa, but through daily living, in Samoa.

Sport is not the purpose of the kilikiti gathering — the celebration of being Samoan is. As with everything else in faa Samoa, that celebration is expressed in carefully defined ways — the discipline of the ritual adding to the sense of community. The pleasure comes from fulfilling worthwhile obligations. It is this quality, difficult for a palagi to explain adequately, which is at the core of kilikiti, and of Samoan strength.

Mark Scott 'Kilikiti', **Metro** May 1987

The spirit of cricket is often expressed in terms of history and tradition.

Playing for your country isn't simply about 'doing your best'. When you wear the silver fern there's a legacy involved, a history which dictates the expectations of players and teams of long ago. Some of the current players scoff at this and I find that distressing. I believe all present players have an obligation to the past; to try to emulate the pride and achievements that have been performed in days gone by...

The players who wear the silver fern now could do a lot worse than draw inspiration from the feats and efforts of Sutcliffe, Donnelly, J.R. Reid, Congdon, Chatfield, Wright and Hadlee. They won the New Zealand game respect and played with pride.

Ken Rutherford and Chris Mirams *A Hell of a Way to Make a Living* (1995)

Tradition and history do not belong only to the players. Cricket's continuity is emphasised whenever a love for the game is passed down from one generation to another.

 It was one of those still, clammy, midsummer afternoons that lie heavy on Auckland, bringing sweat to the brow and a dull pain behind the eyes.

Where we were sitting, half a dozen rows back in the number four stand, there was little movement among the fitful crowd and just the murmur of commentary on muted radios. Not much was happening on the field either, as Derek Randall and Chris Smith meandered their way through the long afternoon and Geoff Howarth used all but four of his team to try to winkle them out on a pitch which had long since gone to sleep. Fielding down in front of us on the boundary, Ewen Chatfield looked as though he too was having trouble staying awake.

Beside me my nine-year-old son and front lawn opponent was doing his best to show an appropriate degree of interest, but his mind was more on his strategy to jump the fence surrounding the ground at the close of play and bag as many players' autographs as possible. For him it was to be a long afternoon indeed.

As the game dozed on, my mind began to stray from the slow rhythm of bat and ball to consider how there was a certain symmetry in play here as England ambled through the low hundreds chasing New Zealand's 496 for 9.

It hadn't always been this way, of course. There had been another time on this ground when another little boy had watched as New Zealand had crashed to being all out for 26 against England. That had been on 28 March 1955; 29 years ago and I had watched from the other side of the ground when I too was nine and had been learning my cricket on the same concrete pitch at Cornwall Park School where my son currently wields the size four bat I bought him last summer. His heroes are Hadlee, Howarth and Cairns. Mine were Sutcliffe and Reid, Frank 'Typhoon' Tyson and Brian Statham. He wants a Lance Cairns 'Excalibur' bat. Mine was autographed by Keith Miller, lovingly soaked each week in linseed oil and taped at its toe. It had a satisfying sweetness.

A year later I had stood not far from where I'm sitting now, atop a banana box in a sea of 60,000 people who'd waited for hours to watch the 1956 Springboks battle Auckland, the Maoris and New Zealand in the magnificent fourth test where Peter Jones scored his memorable try. I remember too, watching in horror as two St John's men half carried 'Tiny' White from the field after he'd been felled by the Springbok forwards in the test. It was as close as Chatfield is today. I was with my father, my uncle and my cousins that day. Two years later, on a February morning not unlike this one had been (I can remember it as though it had been this morning) my father was dead in the front room. He had never played cricket on the front lawn with me. I suppose he'd been too ill all along, although I didn't know that at the time.

And so we drifted into the final hour of play and I considered the continuity of life. It hasn't been a good couple of months. Important things have gone wrong. 'Unhappy differences', as the lawyers put it, have arisen in my marriage. There are rifts and chasms and many things have happened to which I don't know the answers any more, if I ever did. There are difficulties between my son and me. But through it all we're here together, and I feel a strong bond which I hope he still feels for me.

By five to six the desultory Englishmen had stuttered along to 238. Smith had gone, caught behind off Cairns for 91. I'd rather hoped Nicholas would have seen him score a century, but the light is bad and at the end of the over the players break and jog towards the tunnel leading beneath the stand and in no time are gone. Nicholas misses his autographs and I suddenly feel hugely sad for him. We walk in the still afternoon across the crunching gravel back to the car and as we come to the gate I ask him if he's enjoyed himself. He looks up at me and beams and as we cross the road he takes my hand and in doing that he makes my day.

Warwick Roger *Places in the Heart* (1989)

Enjoyment, passion, tradition, continuity...the spirit of cricket cannot be summed up in a few words. For some people, cricket is a game that gets into their very soul...

Groucho Marx was once taken to Lord's to see the opening session of an England v. Australia test cricket match. Play had proceeded for about 40 minutes with the opening batsmen taking the minimum of risks, content to let the ball sail past their bats without offering a stroke. Finally the great man spoke. 'When,' he asked in his gruff voice, cigar clamped between his lips, 'when are they going to start?'

People who know nothing about cricket presume that because it seems slow, and because nothing appears to be happening, that it is a dull, static, anachronistic pastime, fit only for private school boys and older men in their anecdotage. Why else would some unknown and unmissed wit remark that 'cricket was invented by God to teach Englishmen the meaning of the word "eternity"?'.

But take this situation. A batsman is at the crease. He has a weakness for lifting the ball when he drives. He knows this, and the bowler knows it also, and the batsman knows the bowler knows it. Over after over the bowler spins the ball down on a tempting driving length. Over after over the batsman resists the temptation. Then a fieldsman is moved away, leaving a huge gap open for the drive. The change is made quietly without any dramatics. But for the players concerned it is as significant as the pistol introduced in the first act of *Hedda Gabler* which the audience knows will be fired at the end of the play.

What does the batsman do? Does he take up the challenge?

The ball curves down towards him, seemingly on the same full length as all the others. This ball, however, has been held back, just a bit, and drops a fraction shorter than the other balls. The batsman sees its generous length, drives at it, mishits and sends the ball swirling to cover.

On his way back to the pavilion, he slams his bat against his pad in frustration at falling into the trap set for him. As Arthur Milton, the phlegmatic England opener, used to say about the taxing art of cricket: 'It's all a matter of inches — those between your ears.'

To the casual, uninformed spectator, nothing very much has happened. A batsman who was shaping up competently enough suddenly had a rush of blood to the head and was out, caught. In fact, an intense, exciting moral drama had played itself out. A drama of temptation, pressure and ambition as old as the Biblical story of Adam, Eve and the apple. The knowledgeable spectator sees all these cricket dramas, the games within the game, and savours them as one of the Joys of cricket.

Sir Robert Menzies, who can be forgiven many things as a politician because he loved cricket, has pointed out that cricket is 'the mother of great traditions. It dwells in the eye and in the blood. The relative slowness of its tempo induces observations and enables subtleties to be seen and noted.'

The point is that the slowness of cricket is one of its attractions. A rugby test is a sporting one-night stand, over before the game has really started. A cricket test is a long, intricate love affair. There is a time for stroking, for reflection, tension mounts and wanes, climaxes come and go and at the end, no matter what the result, one's life has been enhanced.

To change the metaphor, the Joy of cricket is that the game, at its best, takes the form of a great panoramic novel. with several dozen characters observed over a long period of time (the umpires are crucial to the action, too) so that their foibles and mannerisms come through. The best matches have a strong plot line and within this basic structure any number of minor climaxes and set pieces — the opening overs, for instance, when the new ball flashes off the pitch and a hush comes over the ground as Richard Hadlee, say, with his mechanical menace, comes in to bowl — is a classic that never fails to thrill.

The genius of the game, though, is that while it unravels like a great novel, each ball is a complete and perfect short story. So the game possesses a contrapuntal tension. There is a long, extended plot line as the innings builds up and, at the same time, the sustaining interest of each particular ball. Neville Cardus, the greatest of cricket writers, once reported how he went outside for a breather while England was batting on a typical 1930s shirt-front wicket. In the few minutes he was away, Bill O'Reilly had snatched three wickets turning the game away.

Every ball is a potential turning point, or a potential moment of exquisite beauty as someone like Martin Crowe leans into an on-drive and, in Cardus' description of the way Charles Macartney used to play, 'dismisses it from his presence'.

It is no more possible to leave a cricket ground without lingering to see 'one more ball,' than it is for someone who is deeply in love to walk away from that loved person and not turn back for a last, lingering look.

Spiro Zavos 'The Joy of Cricket', **Metro** December 1987

SIX

IN CASE YOU WERE
WONDERING

My name, I admit, is unknown in the highest cricketing circles, but I have had my glorious moments in the game.

There was, for example, the day I bowled the England captain for a duck. Not in a match of course: more in a free-for-all on the practice pitch when the 1957 England women's touring team came to our school on a goodwill visit. In those days I was the Second Eleven's secret weapon, a bowler of impeccable direction but such temptingly slow pace that opponents could seldom resist the urge to hit me out of the park. I could always rely on picking up two or three wickets an innings, from miscued hook shots, or agricultural slogs that failed to connect. When the great Mary Duggan took guard, however, I certainly did not expect to succeed. A few Gavin Larsen-like hops and a whirl of the arm later, and the ball was on its way. It hit the ground, bounced no more than a couple of inches and shot through underneath her elegantly positioned bat. Not exactly a delivery to be proud of — but then, how many of you have ever bowled to an England captain?

Shortly afterwards, I reached the dizzying heights of the college First Eleven. This was a rather better achievement than it sounds, for the team played in the senior competition in those days, and was captained by an extremely astute and somewhat forbidding individual who was already honing the skills that would make her a highly successful captain of New Zealand. Pat McKelvey did not exactly advise me to forget about bowling — she just never gave me the ball and I had not enough nerve to ask for it. Instead I batted at six or seven, where I showed the tenacity of a limpet on a rock when a game needed saving but was an utter disaster in a run chase. And I fielded…and fielded…

Fielding was definitely my best cricketing attribute. After an enthusiastic display of chasing and throwing in a trial game I was picked for a representative side. Even at the time I had no clear idea of who I was representing. Was it Wellington Schools? Or Wellington B? What I do remember is travelling some distance from town for a match. The outfield had been cropped by sheep, who had to be chased off before the game could begin, and the grass was slippery with heavy morning dew. I rocketed round the boundary like a demon that day. When stumps were drawn, one of the umpires, a courteous elderly gentleman who perched himself on a shooting stick when officiating at square leg, came over and congratulated me on my fielding and the number of runs I had saved. 'That was Mr Gilligan,' said the coach in awed tones. It was not until much later that I learned Frank Gilligan had played for Oxford University and Essex and that his brothers, Arthur and Harold, had both captained England. Praise from a member of such a distinguished cricketing family was certainly worth having.

I gave up playing cricket when I went to university. Getting my essays in on time was difficult enough, without any sporting distractions. Watching from the boundary proved a great deal less tiring than patrolling it, and I was spared my regular doses of painful sunburn. Listening to cricket broadcasts quickly became a passion — especially when I went to live in England and could enjoy the mellow, measured tones of John Arlott — and I began, also, to fossick in second-hand bookshops for long out-of-print volumes to add to my slowly growing library of cricket books.

The foundations of that collection were laid around the age of 12, when I bought a copy of Ian Peebles' *Talking of Cricket* for sixpence, from the Withdrawn shelf at Wellington Public Library. I had never heard of Peebles, or the players he mentioned, but I enjoyed his book so much that I read it, cover to cover, about six times in succession. It is still in my library, dog-eared and lacking a spine now, but thoroughly well-loved. The power of words to bring players and performances of the past to life has amazed me ever since.

These days I write for a living, not about cricket but about musical and theatrical history. The trouble is that my love of cricket keeps breaking into my real work, particularly in summer when the endless fascination of *Sports' Roundup* causes me many a missed deadline. Sometimes, when I am researching, my eye is caught by an interesting cricketing title and I cannot resist the temptation to have a look at it. This is how I came across a slim volume called *The Ladies Guide to Cricket by a Lover of Both* at the Alexander Turnbull Library. It was published in Auckland in 1883 and consists of conversations between two cricketing gentlemen and two ladies whom they are instructing in the finer points of the game. The anonymous author includes a glossary of cricketing slang and it is fascinating to see which terms have remained current and which are now completely obsolete. I like the word tice for an overpitched ball, but I am not sure the Cambridge-poke and Harrow-drive stand much chance of revival.

The Ladies Guide to Cricket includes this little poem *Ten Ways to Get Out*. I could not find a place for it anywhere else, so I thought it might make a good ending.

Ten Ways to Get Out

Careful and clever that batsman must be
Who wishes to tot up a century.
Ten different dangers hedge him about
By any of which he may be put out.
First 'bowled', *second* 'caught', and *third* 'leg before',
A fate that most batsmen dislike and deplore.
The *fourth* is 'run out', deemed very bad cricket;
The *fifth* if he clumsily 'hit his own wicket'.
Stumped is the *sixth*, the *seventh* we'll call
Foolishly touching or handling the ball.
Eighth, is the striker 'should hit the ball twice'
With malice prepense — a pestilent vice,
Ninth if he purposely spoils a fair catch
While running — and *tenth*, the last of the batch,
When jacket or hat, propelled by the gale,
Touches the wicket displacing a bail!

Anonymous ***The Ladies Guide to Cricket*** (1883)

ACKNOWLEDGEMENTS

The publishers are grateful to the following authors, publishers and copyright holders for their permission to reproduce copyright material:

Chapter 1

Jeremy Coney *The Playing Mantis* (Moa, 1985) © Hodder Moa Beckett; Ashley Mallet *Clarrie Grimmett: The Bradman of Spin* (University of Queensland Press, 1993) © University of Queensland Press; Glenn Turner *My Way* (Hodder and Stoughton, 1975) © Hodder Moa Beckett; Bert Sutcliffe *Between Overs* (Whitcombe & Tombs, 1963) © Penguin Books; Bruce Edgar with David Roberts *Bruce Edgar: An Opener's Tale* (1987) © Bruce Edgar; Spiro Zavos 'Facing the Giants' (*New Zealand Listener* 3 March 1984) © Spiro Zavos; Ian Smith, as told to Roger Brittenden *Smithy: Just a Drummer in the Band* (Moa, 1991) © Hodder Moa Beckett; Ken Rutherford and Chris Mirams *A Hell of a Way to Make a Living* (Hodder Moa Beckett, 1995) © Hodder Moa Beckett; J.R. Reid *Sword of Willow* (A.H. & A.W. Reed, 1962) © Reed Publishing NZ.

Chapter 2

R.T. Brittenden *New Zealand Cricketers* (A.H. & A.W. Reed, 1961) © Reed Publishing NZ; Denys Rowbottom 'Great Batting at Aigburth', reprinted in Kenneth Gregory *In Celebration of Cricket* (Pavilion, 1978) © Guardian News Service Ltd; T.P. McLean 'Aussie Greats Remember Kiwi Cricket Stars' (*New Zealand Herald*, 19 November 1966) © *New Zealand Herald*; John Woodcock 'Turner: Man of Principle and a Perfectionist' (*The Times*, 2 June 1982) © Times Newspapers Ltd, 1982; Ron Palenski 'A bit of cricket died the day Crowe called it quits' (*Dominion*, 18 January 1996) © *The Dominion*; Joseph Romanos 'Crème de la cricket' (*New Zealand Listener*, 13 July 1996) © Joseph Romanos; Stewart Kinross *Please to Remember* (A.H. & A.W. Reed, 1963) © Reed Publishing NZ.

Chapter 3

John Arlott *John Arlott's Cricket Journal* (William Heinemann Ltd, 1958) © Reed Consumer Books Ltd; Peter Roebuck *Great Innings* (Anaya Publications Ltd, 1989) © Collins & Brown; J.R. Reid *A Million Miles of Cricket* (A.H. & A.W. Reed, 1966) © Reed Publishing NZ; Richard Hadlee with Richard Becht *Rhythm and Swing* (Moa, 1989) © Hodder Moa Beckett; D.J. Cameron 'The Test with Everything' (*New Zealand Herald*, 19 February 1973) © *New Zealand Herald*; Bert Sutcliffe *Between Overs* (Whitcombe & Tombs, 1963) © Penguin Books; D.J. Cameron *Memorable Moments in New Zealand Sport* (Moa, 1979) © Hodder Moa Beckett; D.J. Cameron *Caribbean Crusade* (Hodder and Stoughton, 1972) © Hodder Moa Beckett; J.R. Reid *Sword of Willow* (A.H. & A.W. Reed, 1962) © Reed Publishing NZ.

Chapter 4

R.T. Brittenden *Great Days in New Zealand Cricket* (A.H. & A.W. Reed, 1958) © Reed Publishing NZ; Tom Hyde 'Men in White Coats' (*Metro*, February 1989) © *Metro* Magazine; Graham Hutchins *The Howarth Years* (John McIndoe, 1985) © Graham Hutchins; Barry Hawkins 'Among the Fans on the Basin's Bank' (*Evening Post*, 25 June 1991) © *The Evening Post*; Peter Calder 'King Lear, Michelangelo — and Smithy' (*New Zealand Herald*, 24 February 1990) © *New Zealand Herald*.

Chapter 5

Elizabeth Smither 'Cricket' (*Metro*, March 1995) © *Metro* Magazine; John Wright with Paul Thomas *Christmas in Rarotonga* (Moa, 1989) © Hodder Moa Beckett; R.T. Brittenden *New Zealand Cricketers* (A.H. & A.W. Reed, 1961) © Reed Publishing NZ; Warwick Roger 'Coarse Cricket' (*Metro*, February 1989) © *Metro* Magazine; Frank Stark 'Yes, but is it cricket?' (*New Zealand Listener*, 11 August 1984) © *New Zealand Listener*; Mark Scott 'Kilikiti' (*Metro*, May 1987) © *Metro* Magazine; Ken Rutherford and Chris Mirams *A Hell of a Way to Make a Living* (Hodder Moa Beckett, 1995) © Hodder Moa Beckett; Warwick Roger *Places in the Heart* (Century Hutchinson, 1989) © Warwick Roger; Spiro Zavos 'The Joy of Cricket' (*Metro*, December 1987) © *Metro* Magazine.

While every attempt has been made to contact copyright holders and secure permission to reproduce copyright material, it has not always been possible to do so. Copyright holders of the following material are invited to contact the publisher.

R.C. Robertson-Glasgow *Cricket Prints* (T. Werner Laurie Ltd, 1943); Walter Hammond *Cricket My World* (Stanley Paul, 1948); Alan W. Mitchell *Cricketing Companions* (T. Werner Laurie Ltd, 1950); John Arlott *The Echoing Green* (Longmans, Green & Co. Ltd, 1952); A.A. Thomson *Cricket: The Great Captains* (Stanley Paul, 1965); Simon Wilde *Letting Rip* (H.F. & G. Witherby, 1994); John Arlott 'New Zealand Power' (*Wisden Cricket Monthly*, April 1983); Ian Peebles *Talking of Cricket* (Museum Press, 1953); E.W. Swanton *Cricket from all Angles* (Michael Joseph, 1962); Patrick Smith (editor) *The Age World Cup Cricket 1992* (The Five Mile Press, 1992); Anthony Meredith *Summers in Winter* (The Kingswood Press, 1990); Nancy Joy *Maiden Over* (Sporting Handbooks Ltd, 1950); Don Mosey *The Best Job in the World* (Pelham Books, 1985); Paul Huggett 'In the Box Seat' (*New Zealand Listener*, 11 March 1991).